The Founder's Manifest

*For Anyone Starting
a New Business*

The Founder's Manifest

*For Anyone Starting
a New Business*

My-Tien Vo

Nine Spheres
2017

NINE SPHERES
The Founder's Manifest
For Anyone Starting a New Business
My-Tien Vo

Copyeditor: Sarah C. Baldwin
Cover Designer: Laura J. Rinaldi

First printing 2017; updated January 2019.
Printed in the United States of America

Published in the United States of America by Nine Spheres
ISBN-13: 978-0-9982976-0-6

1. Founder Development. 2. Founder Competency. 3. Founder's Integrated Approach. 4. Founder's Integrated Mindset. 5. Founder Leadership. 6. Startups. 7. New Business. 8. Entrepreneurship. 9. The Immediacy Mindset.

To my parents

To my parents

Contents

Foreword

The Founder's Manifest focuses on the entrepreneur rather than product or mechanics of entrepreneurship. Most startups find their product needs redesign once it's on the market. The well-regarded "lean startup" approach focuses on how best to do this. Mechanics are important, and the book mentions them, but My-Tien Vo wisely recognizes that the founder's approach is usually the determining factor in a successful venture. Experienced investors bet on the jockey rather than the horse.

Two strengths of My-Tien's book are conversational writing style and thought-provoking exercises. Her writing will draw you in, as if she were sitting across the table from you. Exercises will push you to think about whether you have the temperament or "stomach" to be an entrepreneur. They'll also help you recognize skills you already possess and training you still need. I respect the advice this book gives: to be an entrepreneur, one has to be determined, prepared, self-reliant, and tough. No pandering here with vague assurances that "everything will work out fine."

Encouragement of original thought is another strength of the book. You don't have to agree with everything, but you'll be better for having thought critically. You'll benefit from dissecting each exercise.

It has been a pleasure for me watching My-Tien's career. She was a very good student of mine at Brown University. Not only did she learn quickly, she was resourceful and creative. As good entrepreneurs do, she recognized opportunities. She differed from many students by thinking through a plan to leverage opportunities. Since graduation, she has been a successful entrepreneur and simultaneously an adviser/coach to entrepreneurs. Besides being a writer, she is an effective editor. I personally have worked with her to create an important and original platform (brownhen.org) where entrepreneurs share insights and stories. I've worked with her to establish a vehicle for entrepreneurs to meet face-to-face. I marvel at her energy and determination.

My-Tien's experience as an entrepreneur, adviser, and organizer enrich this book. This narrative is seasoned with vignettes about things she knows. She writes from the heart. You'll gain from reading what she has to say.

Barrett Hazeltine, Ph.D.
Associate Dean of the College (1972-1992)
Professor Emeritus of Engineering
Adjunct Professor
Brown University
Providence, Rhode Island
March 2017

Acknowledgments

Writing a book is a solitary act that requires inspiration and nourishment from many sources. Many heartfelt thanks to the following individuals for their support, time and valuable advice: my parents, Gregory Baldwin, Sarah C. Baldwin, Randy Haykin, Barrett Hazeltine, Fredric A. Leslie, Laura J. Rinaldi, Martin Schnitzer, and James H. Sutton.

Introduction

You've been nurturing a dream of starting your own company and unearthed an idea that excites you. Now you wonder how to proceed. I've written this book to help you do that.

My first goal is to show you how to perform due diligence—research and assessment—so you can decide if you are ready to create a company. My second goal is to help you prepare for your founder role, if you decide to proceed.

I've spent two decades in the startup trenches with founders and startup teams; I can speak to entrepreneurial success and failure. I felt compelled to write this book and help first-time founders prepare well for their startup because I've witnessed inexperienced product-centric founders committing the same missteps time and again. I believe it's time for a new startup model.

What This Book Is About

The Founder's Manifest focuses on you, the founder; it's meant to guide your development. It introduces an integrated mindset and approach to help entrepreneurs develop Founder Competency—skills and qualities that a new founder must possess. This reflects my belief that the best way to prepare for an entrepreneurial journey is to focus on yourself first; you need to develop as a competent and self-reliant founder before immersion in product development.

Why Focus on the Founder

The founder is creator and product originator. The more qualified and prepared, the better the venture and the product. As such, a founder shoulders immense responsibility and wields great influence over outcomes.

Picture your entrepreneurial journey as a sea voyage. Your product is your offering to the world. First you need to build it. Then you need a vessel to transport your cargo and a qualified skipper at the helm.

As founder, you are the captain. You need to be competent before setting sail. You don't have to be an expert in how to tie rigging, but you do need to know seamanship. This means knowing how to navigate; hire and manage your crew; allocate and monitor resources; solve unanticipated problems; handle rough waters and storms; and ensure that your cargo and people reach port.

If you're like most first-time founders, you probably possess expertise in your profession and have enthusiasm for your new business idea. Like new founders, you want to devote all your energy to developing your product and getting it to market, and everything else is afterthought.

Inventors are driven by a product-centric mindset: create product, then find investors to finance it. The current investor community also favors this product-centric approach, so this has been consecrated as the default startup model.

New founders who start with this mindset don't recognize that they need to know how to build their product, and how to build and run their business. They don't realize that a product idea—no matter how good or great or unique or revolutionary—will not see long life if its founder executes poorly.

Why Read This Book

The Founder's Manifest will help you develop as a founder—one who is responsible for both product and venture. The one constant you'll always have is you. It will show you how to invest time and energy in your most important asset—you—so that the more qualified and prepared you are, the more helpful and resourceful you will be—the greater your chance of success.

This book will raise your awareness of your critical role as founder, and help you develop as an individual and as a founder. It will also help you augment your worth as founder throughout your entrepreneurial journey. Many first-time founders give little thought to their own worth and unknowingly give away too much of their company in return for too little.

This book's integrated mindset and approach to founder development reflect my belief that "proper planning prevents poor performance." For new founders, this means developing competency before diving too deeply into product development. Many first-time founders already possess some of these core skills and qualities, and can learn to refine or develop others that are articulated in this book. No other books have focused on helping aspiring founders learn to perceive themselves as an integrated and self-reliant individual about to embark on a new path and a competent skipper captaining his/her first ship.

Proper planning entails continual reflection, assessment, articulation, decision-making, and execution. One needs to understand the big picture, key issues, and how to execute details. In the frenzy of a start-up, planning can avoid chaos and breakdown. This book will help you prepare so you can assume the helm confidently.

Who Should Read This Book

The Founder's Manifest is for aspiring founders of any age, race, gender, creed, background, or ability to learn. It's for anyone who contemplates starting his or her own business—whether profit or non-profit, whether it's a neighborhood shop owner, a service provider, a manufacturing firm, or a tech startup. This includes:

- Those who don't have time or money for entrepreneurial degree programs—professionals, breadwinners, working spouses, stay-at-home parents, single parents, veterans, and retirees.

- Seasoned professionals with deep expertise in their field but no experience in starting and running a new company.

- College students, recent graduates, MBA candidates, as well as graduate students.

What You Can Achieve with This Book

An integrated mindset and approach—toward your own development, your product, and your business—will help you be strategic and tactical as you make decisions. An awareness of your importance and worth as founder, and an understanding of how you can build your capacity throughout your venture. These will protect you and your creation. *The Founder's Manifest* will also give you:

- Knowledge of how you can develop founder competency—including self-reliance—before assuming the helm as captain.

- Knowledge of how you can plan and build your product as well as your business. With an integrated mindset, this can help you avoid wasting energy, time, talent, money, and other resources.

- Familiarity with the entrepreneurial landscape. This includes available resources and familiarity with the prevailing attitudes toward startups and founders. Having a clear idea of the landscape can help you make more astute decisions for yourself, team, and operation while avoiding missteps.

- Development of your own manifest, which will serve as your own field guide, Go-To resource, and Survival Kit.

Each founder is unique. What you bring on board and how you navigate will be unique. You shape your venture. You need to train and develop yourself into the most qualified captain that you can be. No one can do this for you. Only you can decide how well prepared you will be. How you start will affect how you perform—and how you end.

How to Use This Book

This book is a guide to developing founder competency. You'll find Founder Insights, Startup Anecdotes, and more than 60 exercises to help you complete a thorough due diligence, including self-examination, to determine readiness and prepare well.

Read this book through for an overview. Then re-read it more methodically. Questions and exercises will help you think through important issues that each new founder needs to address.

Use a notebook or a laptop to capture your answers while reading and working through exercises. Create your manifest with your answers and insights. Monitor the following and devise your action plan:

- Issues to reflect on and assess
- Skills you need to develop
- Resources you need to research and allocate
- Tools for your Survival Kit

You may find some exercises useful and others irrelevant, based on your experience. Skip areas you have mastered.

Some questions may be easy; others require effort to answer. Some may even raise more questions. Don't be frustrated if you don't have answers. I've asked myself many questions over and over. Sometimes, it takes time to gain clarity.

Some questions may make you uncomfortable because they hit weak spots you've managed to avoid so far. Pay attention to those that make you want to say, "I dislike sales (or accounting or public relations)." When you find yourself thinking like this, recognize that these signal potential problems, if you don't attend to them before starting out. Don't avoid them; commit to addressing them before you begin your entrepreneurial journey.

Be honest regarding your abilities and limitations. Identify what you're willing to do. By knowing before you start, you can: 1) leverage personal and professional strengths, 2) monitor what you need to refine, 3) develop competency where needed, and 4) hire someone with competency or expertise to help you where you may be lacking. If you have a job description with seven things on it and someone does five well, give thanks, and hire that individual.

Keep the following in mind. We absorb information and learn in our own way. Move at your own pace. The more time and energy you devote to your development now, the richer your self-discovery and preparation will be later on. New self-awareness and understanding will fortify you in your founder role. Insights gained from your own manifest will support you throughout your venture.

A clarification regarding definitions:

- "Venture" refers to the entirety of your entrepreneurial odyssey.

- "Startup" means a new entity that may be profit or nonprofit.

- "Product" means physical product, service, or software tool.

- "Operation" means: 1) a physical and/or virtual office; 2) marketing, sales, engineering, legal, and financial departments created to support your product and business; and 3) individuals who are responsible for various roles.

- "Infrastructure" refers to the framework (including business structures: research, marketing, sales, engineering, and legal), systems, and processes that support your operation.

The Path Not Taken

I wrote this book with the goal of helping you to move forward with your business idea. Moving forward means taking the next steps to prepare yourself as founder.

Moving forward can also mean that after reading this book and performing your due diligence, you conclude that you're not ready to leave your current job and life to start down a new career path this year, or that the entrepreneurial life is not for you. That's okay, too.

There's value in taking time to reacquaint yourself with your past and bring all that you are into the present. Furthermore, there's value in conducting self-examination and concluding that a path doesn't feel right because of an untenable product idea, lack of experience, resources, and/or consumer interest. Once you've gone through this initial process and obtained solid understanding of what's required to prepare and start well, you can be at peace with your decision to not go forward.

If you do decide to assume the helm as founder, you still need to keep learning and growing.

Throughout this book, you will find startup anecdotes to illustrate where things went right or wrong. For privacy reasons, I've changed names of founders, co-founders, and startups.

So, how to proceed? First, familiarize yourself with where you're going.

Chapter I:
Study the Waters You Plan to Navigate

You are about to commit to a new business idea, role, and life path. This requires time, energy, and resources. To reach your destination, you need to investigate where you're going and prepare for the journey, including planning for emergencies.

The idea of an entrepreneur blazing a trail is Romantic. In today's frenetic and unforgiving business world, you don't need to reinvent the wheel. You can avoid common mistakes, if you make time to identify places where others have run aground. You need to be as well prepared as you can be before starting out. Once you embarked on your journey, you'll need to use resources efficiently.

Many starting businesses have tunnel vision from the start: they operate from inside the product bubble. They spend little time researching the new environment and its inherent challenges. They didn't take a wide view from the start, and that led to poor performance.

To write this book, I researched like an aspiring founder, digging deep to uncover what is available. Numerous visits to the public library and bookstores, and online searches generated a long list of book titles, interviews, articles, and blog posts. You may need to do this, too.

The following shows insights gained from research and experience as a serial founder and entrepreneur. I share them to increase your understanding of the entrepreneurial scene so you can prepare and navigate as well as you can.

Recognize It's a Great Time to Be an Entrepreneur

If you want to start a new business, there has never been a better time to be "a person who undertakes or controls a business or enterprise and bears the risk of profit or loss—an entrepreneur."[1]

As a new founder, you have many more resources at your disposal for starting and building a company efficiently and quickly than those who did this even five years ago.

Access to Resources

You have easy access to an abundance of books, interviews, articles, and blog posts on how to start a new business. You can gain insights at startup networking events, meet-ups, forums, and lectures offered by your local Small Business Association (SBA).

You're able to set up a new business more efficiently than ever. You have immediate access to tools for creating a new business identity: accounts, e-commerce websites, marketing tools, sales tools, and customer service tools. The application process for new business licenses are more streamlined. Find forms at your local Chamber of Commerce's website and your state government's website.

You can acquire formal education. Since the 1990s, entrepreneurship has gained traction as a career path as well as a discipline. Academic institutions offer bachelor and master's degree programs in entrepreneurship. The Princeton Review tracks and ranks the top 50 U.S. programs.

You have a multitude of financing resources: SBA loans, credit union loans, commercial bank loans, angel investors, crowd funding, and venture capitalists.

No Formal Training Required

No formal training, certification, or licensing is required to "practice" as a founder. Accountants, lawyers, physicians, and professors must obtain credentials in advance and cannot practice until certified; they also learn on the job. A license ensures high and enforced standards of minimum performance; this protects the public. But there are no legal barriers to becoming an entrepreneur. Anyone can start a business and learn by doing. That's the upside.

No Protection Against Failure

The flip side is you can set off on your venture even if you lack skills and qualifications. Your only assurance is what you know and what you can do.

You may have a head start if you've enrolled in an entrepreneurship program, if you've grown up around entrepreneurs, or if you have start-up experience. But there's a difference between joining a startup as an employee and founding a startup. It takes an array of knowledge, experience, wisdom, and skill sets to launch and build a business—whether it's brick-and-mortar retailer, manufacturer of goods, service-oriented firm, or an online store.

While many first-time founders can possess knowledge and skills that enable them to start a business, most lack experience and training to run one. I was an untrained founder. I've also worked with smart professionals in hospitality, law, software, retail services, healthcare, and professional services who failed as founders.

Founder Insights

Today, there's no entry barrier to becoming a founder. The quality of founders varies because there are no standardized requirements or license to practice entrepreneurship. If you haven't had any founder experience, you'll want to increase your chance of success by researching thoroughly and preparing as well as you can for your founder role and entrepreneurial journey.

- Read books, articles, and interviews on starting a business. Borrow from your local library; purchase books. Gather insights and advice from those who have done it and want to share.

- Research tools and services that will help you build your business.

- Take classes or study on your own to develop competency in your weak areas.

- Volunteer or work as an intern or apprentice to gain experience in the industry niche in which you intend to create your new business.

- Gain experience by working for an established business and/or a startup before striking out on your own.

There's no single successful startup playbook. You must research and create your own map.

Don't become a failure because of ignorance and lack of preparation.

Study Failures to Learn From Others' Mistakes

According to the Kauffman Index of Startup Activity, 2016 saw an increase in entrepreneurial activity; more than 550,000 individuals became new business owners each month.[2] Yet, seven out of ten new employer firms survive at least two years, half at least five years, a third at least ten years, and a quarter for fifteen years or more.[3] These failure rates have remained unchanged over time, according to the SBA, which tracks business formation and closure.

Why do so many fail? There's a long list of reasons. Here are the main reasons, based on my experience. You can avoid them if you plan well.

Lack of Core Founder Qualities and Skills

Some founders lack founder competency, which include self-reliance, self-awareness, self-management, communications skills, relationship management skills, and crisis management skills. Some are great at launching their products, but fail miserably at building their companies. When they encounter operational glitches, they balk or they bail.

Failure to Assume Responsibility for Both Operation and Product

Some founders are so focused on product they neglect essential components of their operation, which include team management (making sure people are challenged, happy in their work, and compensated properly), brand development, marketing strategy, sales team training, accounting, and customer support.

When about to launch product, they realize these components aren't in place. Their new sales team members haven't received any marketing collateral, sales tools, and training. They haven't set up a customer support process. The result is delayed product launch.

Some founders count on a huge sales opportunity that will bring in much needed revenue. When the opportunity surfaces, they can't seize it because they haven't allocated sufficient human resources to support a large-scale operation.

Poor Budgeting

Some entrepreneurs don't budget well and run out of funds. Common reasons are: 1) they underestimate time and resources to develop product and run a business, 2) they don't assess needs appropriately and spend on unnecessary expenses while neglecting highest priorities, and 3) they underestimate the time it takes to generate revenues and to raise money.

Lack of Industry Experience

Some founders create a product from personal experience, but lack industry experience. They have no idea how bureaucratic starting a company is until mired in legal requirements and environmental regulations; then they conclude that compliance would be too costly for a bootstrapping business. Other founders don't realize they're offering a product to an industry with high barriers to entry; one with long sales and approval cycles; or a late-adopter industry that is uncomfortable with new ways of solving problems.

The Entrepreneurial Life Didn't Suit Them

Some founders discover they prefer being part of a larger enterprise rather than working as their own boss and shouldering responsibility of their own business. Others discover it's lonely and exhausting being their own number-one cheerleader 24/7. Some decide they prefer a steady income. Most entrepreneurs close shop after four or five years and return to former industries.

Founder Insights

It's difficult to replicate a winning formula because you'll never get the exact same environment, individuals, conditions, or resources.

It's easy to make mistakes due to inexperience, ignorance, or poor preparation. Being aware of reasons for failure can help avoid them. Throughout this book, you'll find stories of success and failure. Keep them in mind. As you complete exercises, note what triggers discomfort or fear in you, whether it's team management, marketing, financial planning, sales, or customer service. These may be areas that you feel like avoiding when you should be noting them as weak spots and adding them to your list of competencies to develop.

Research Widely and Keep Only What's Useful

You have easy access to a multitude of startup resources: books, interviews, magazine articles, TV shows, podcasts, and blog postings. Use them, and conduct in-depth due diligence before embarking on any entrepreneurial voyage.

When you conduct online research, you'll find articles and postings like "How to Start a Business in Ten Days" and "Three Great Criteria for a Successful Startup" or "Five Tips to a Great Startup Strategy." If you review some of these writers' bios, you'll see that many possess startup experience, but are not founders themselves.

Not long ago, I read an Entrepreneur magazine supplement titled "Entrepreneur's Instant Startup Guide." The table of contents listed the following sections: Planning, Money, Websites, Marketing, Networking, and Customers. Under Planning was, "How to write a business plan and get going."[4]

This Guide promotes the same incomplete planning process that contributes to failure. There's infinitely more to Planning than "write a business plan and get going." All founders should focus on self-assessment, purpose, vision, values, habits, product definition, market research, concept testing, and brand development.

Seasoned entrepreneurs will tell you there's so much thinking and planning in starting a new venture that you'll need more than ten days. When you don't invest time to prepare carefully and create the proper engine and systems to move forward, you'll pay for it later.

Founder Insights

Avoid advice that endorses a "quick start" or an "instant launch." Be wary of any resource that offers the "ultimate guide" or "the only startup resource you'll ever need." No single startup model works for all. Just as you are a unique individual with your own sets of experiences, belies, values, and goals, so too will your founder development and startup path be unique. Customize your approach. Educate yourself using an array of resources, and extract what resonates with your values and vision for your entrepreneurial journey.

Note a source's professional background and credentials. How much startup experience does this person possess? Does this individual possess founder experience? There's a marked difference between team member and founder. Those respective roles will give you vastly different startup perspectives. Is the author's industry background relevant to you? Does this person's value system align with yours? What resonates with you? Does this person appear to be someone you can trust? Consult widely but be selective.

Recognize the Immediacy Mindset

Recognize how the Immediacy Mindset affects you as founder and know what to do about it. While you dream about launching an overnight success like Snapchat or Instagram, you need to be realistic. The entrepreneurial path is not a straight line from A to B. It's more like from A to Z by way of J, Q, and L.

The Immediacy Mindset

It pervades all aspects of our lives. It holds us hostage, yet we're unaware of its effects.

For businesses, the Immediacy Mindset dictates the creation and delivery of products directly and quickly. It requires that information be served up as soon as possible—preferably five minutes ago and in a format that's easy to consume. It compels a business to perform ever faster to stay competitive and relevant. As a result, employees (retail workers, plant operation managers, programmers, or sales directors) are on a never-ending train of immediate demands.

For customers, the Immediacy Mindset has created an expectation of instant gratification. Customers are used to immediate access, service, and delivery. The upside for customers is that companies continually compete to provide better products, faster service, and enhanced support. The downside is that sometimes, service and/or product quality are compromised for the sake of speedy delivery and response.

For all of us, the Immediacy Mindset creates pressure to perform speedily, digest quickly, decide instantly, and respond promptly. Thanks to smart technologies, we live with this embedded pressure 24/7/365.

Here are ways the Immediacy Mindset adds a frenzy to the entrepreneurial landscape:

First, many new business models are based on providing immediate access, prompt service, and speedy delivery. So founders and their startup teams live under constant pressure to act fast.

Second, some founders believe their offering is cutting-edge, so they rush to lead and stay ahead of competition. Building a product and a company is complex, and demands work in brand development, product strategy, customer service, human resources allocation, law, budget allocation, sales strategy, and more. Each requires in-depth research, analysis, reflection, and study. When a founder rushes to launch product to "stay ahead," he often misses finer points that come back to haunt him later. It might even cost him customers or financing.

Third, some come from structured work environments where they were responsible only for their respective functional responsibilities as sales director, industrial designer, product manager, scientist, or chef. At the end of a workday, they could go home and not worry about their business.

Many founders get overwhelmed by their to-do lists because they're responsible for company culture, their own performance, talent management, operation, business development, marketing, financial management, and so on. There's relentless pressure to stay on top of product development and market trends, to absorb and digest news efficiently, to make decisions quickly, and to respond promptly to all team members, suppliers, and strategic partners. They don't know how to get off the ship for shore leave.

Finally, some founders suffer from "Keeping up with the Joneses," especially in startup incubators like RocketSpace or Plug & Play Tech Centers. These environments are great for immediate feedback and support from other entrepreneurs. But when everyone around is drowning in activity, there's pressure to do likewise.

Founder Insights

How can you avoid succumbing to this Immediacy Mindset? Make "Immediacy" work for you. How we respond to this mindset is related to how we value our own and others' time, how we prioritize, and how we plan.

Review how you manage your time. If you find yourself struggling with prioritization, if you're always stressed because you're always over-extended, it is time to assess and refine how you manage your time. There are books, articles, and workshops devoted to time management. Read widely to discover the approach that suits you.

Pace yourself. Avoid shifting into Overdrive as soon as you've hired a new team member. Acknowledge what you (and your team) can and cannot do within certain time constraints. This doesn't mean you shouldn't push yourself to achieve excellence. But you must pace yourself. Avoid crashing and burning. Allocate time for recharge.

If you can, avoid investing all of your energy and resources in one client or one project. Always allocate some resources for new opportunities.

Be realistic about your deadline commitments. Build in extra time for yourself and your team because everything always takes longer than planned, especially if several individuals are involved. This includes bringing new members on board: allow for sufficient training time. Avoid team burnout due to unreasonable deadlines. Take care of your people before your customers. If you don't, you'll find yourself with high turnover, and no one to accompany you in your venture.

Knowing how much time and resources are needed to deliver a quality product enables you to meet with a client—prepared.

Manage expectations. Within your company, you need to set a deadline that you can meet, with time to perform quality control without killing yourself and your team. With clients and external collaborators, you need to commit to a date and honor it. If you find that you cannot, you must communicate this development immediately to reset your team's and your strategic partner's expectations. You'll reduce stress for all involved when you manage expectations realistically.

Managing others' expectations is self-empowering. It will keep you from becoming a hostage to the Immediacy Mindset. Fear of losing an account often leads founders to cave in to unreasonable customer expectations. Yet in any working relationship, even with one's most difficult strategic partner, there's always room for negotiation regarding the delivery date.

Know the difference between urgent and important, perfect and complete. Not every request or deadline is urgent. Not every task needs to be done perfectly.

Beware the Herd Mentality

Founders are thought of as people who eschew working for others or following in another's footsteps. Yet many don't blaze their own trail. When it comes to product ideas, business model, crowd sourcing, tech tools, even open-space offices, many follow the herd.

At any moment in time, there's a "next big thing" product. In the dot-com days of the early 1990s, everyone rushed to create an e-commerce business. Next came social networking platforms and a photo-sharing phase. Then came frenzy to build online deal marketplaces and a rush to create apps for smart phones, mobile payments, cloud storage, security services, wearables, and robotics. Offline, we've observed new diets (gluten free, raw, and Paleo) and food crazes (bubble teas, cronuts, sushi doughnuts, and ramen burgers).

Many who followed the herd and pursued trendy products or services failed. Here are some reasons. One, they'd missed the boat: consumer interest in the "next big thing" waned by the time they launched a similar offering. Two, founders were "in it for the money" and not emotionally connected to their product. When they encountered engineering glitch, talent management crises, or budget challenges, many lacked faith and drive to find knowledge, skill, and resources needed to persevere and succeed.

Founder Insights

Start with a process or an approach proven to be effective and efficient for you. Don't reject "traditional" ways of doing things just because they're traditional. Examine merits of any business model, hiring approach, business process, or technological tools that you are considering. Research benefits, flaws, and costs; assess if they're right for you, your team, and your customers. Figure out what you and your business need, and avoid the herd.

Examine Merits in the Product-Centric Model

The dance between entrepreneur and his financier has always existed. Entrepreneur invents a product and tries to find capital to build and sell it to grow his business. Even in ancient Egypt, Babylonia, Greece, and Rome, an entrepreneur could borrow from private bankers.[5]

Today's entrepreneur has multiple sources of financing. The investment community has expanded to include friends and family, angel investors, SBA and government loans, commercial banks, credit unions, crowd sourcing, and venture capitalists. But the burden still rests on the inventor to prove a product is worthwhile.

The product-centric model has been the default for so long that few see any need to dissect and analyze it. But your due diligence should include examining its merits, so you can decide if it's best for you.

What Is the Product-Centric Model and How Do New Founders Employ It

Founders who employ the product-centric model focus energies on building product from the start. They don't need to build a company; their only need is product development. The media, investment community, and tech industries all reinforce this mindset.

In technology, product is everything. In a New York Times article about Google's inner circle, one of the interviewed said CEO Larry Page was focused on products and his direct subordinates were all product people. A former Google executive said Google's executive team comprises product owners, not business people.[6] In 2013, a startup I worked with hired a new developer from Oracle. During our initial interview, this developer told me that at Oracle, "product is king."

Product-centric founders often aim the following goals, in this sequence:

1. Come up with a business idea and build the prototype quickly—by self-financing and/or calling on family and friends.
2. Demonstrate proof of concept: launch it quickly to get traction. Note that traction means different things to different founders (and investors). Some define it as number of products sold. Some focus on the number of unpaid users or monthly active users. Some rely on the number of paid customers and repeat customers.

3. Raise more money and use proceeds to hire more staff, buy more materials, add product features and/or services to keep the venture moving.

4. Build a company, then take it public. For founders who want to flip, the goal is increasing company value to attract a buyer who'll acquire and absorb it, or pay to shut it down.

Why Many Founders Embrace the Product-Centric Model Without Reservation

New founders embrace it unreservedly because it resonates with their instinct to seek the fastest route. At first glance, the product-centric model appears to offer the most efficient route to success.

They embrace it because it reigns as the undisputed startup model, validated by highly publicized mega-successes such as Tumblr, Rockmelt, Instagram, and WhatsApp. Yes, Facebook paid $1 billion in cash and stock to the co-founders of Instagram, which was a less than two years old.[7] Facebook also acquired WhatsApp—an instant messaging application—for an estimated $19.3 billion.[8]

According to Venture Beat, only 41 of 2013's Fortune 500 companies are technology companies.[9] Yet because the media focus on the mega-success stories, this model dominates the entrepreneurial landscape.

What Happens to Many Who Pursue This Model

Though many founders embrace the product-centric model, only a handful of startups experienced mega successes.

Most inexperienced founders falter at Goal No. 2, which is to demonstrate the proof of concept, launch it quickly, and obtain traction (users / paid users / buyers / products sold). Countless founders don't even achieve No. 3, which is to raise money to build the full product and/or expand their operation. The few that manage to obtain some traction and try to achieve No. 3 also fail.

Why? The product-centric model possesses inherent flaws. Seasoned founders have been through the trenches so they know how to avoid missteps. First-time founders—unaware of these pitfalls—often fall into them.

The product-centric model focuses on building the product, not the company.

When inexperienced founders focus on building product instead of a company, they're not seeing the entire venture. They fail to see responsibilities as both founder and product developer.

A qualified founder knows the necessity of investing time into researching and building—or at least developing a blueprint to build an infrastructure that will support both product and operation, from development to growth. Consequently, they treat other integral components (branding, marketing, sales, operations, customer service, accounting, and legal structure) as high priorities and incorporate them into their product development phase.

Less skilled founders spend most of their initial budget on product development; when money is needed for brand development, marketing strategy, new hires, business development and/or customer support, they have little to spare. I've worked with founders who spent 95% of their energy on product development, but didn't spend time researching, thinking, and creating a plan for building their company. When they got in front of potential investors to present their prototype, they were unprepared for questions about brand positioning, marketing strategy, team management, customer support, and even corporate social responsibility.

Embrace the wider view. Build a product and a company—that means infrastructure, standards, and processes. Understand that brand development, pricing strategy, distribution, sales, accounting, and customer support are integral to your product's success.

You should test your product idea to determine if it's marketable, but don't immerse yourself in the product room. Focus on product development only after you have the blueprint to create a foundation and structure to support it. This way, when the time arrives to expand, you don't have to scramble.

Startup Anecdotes

The founder of an online enterprise launched the beta version of their service and garnered some customers. Jay was excited, but had spent no time thinking about how to build an infrastructure to support the budding business.

He rushed out and hired sales managers without an established brand, sales tools, and training guides in place. Sales managers quickly brought in new accounts. Contracts were signed. But the startup didn't have any support staff, so Jay went into a second hiring scramble.

New hires did not receive proper training in sales or customer support because of the rush. Essential functions like brand strategy, marketing, finance, and operations did not exist. Without a well-thought-out customer support system in place, new clients got frustrated because their new issues were not resolved quickly and smoothly.

I came on board to help manage their growing list of clients. I worked with the senior management team to establish processes for client management. We created a guide for customer support and establish communication standards among the engineers, sales people, account managers, and designers.

The venture achieved some stability, but ultimately was absorbed by another company because of numerous reasons: the sales team kept promising more than what the product team could deliver, intensifying client frustration; high employee turnover due to budget cuts; and low company morale due to lack of leadership from an absentee founder.

Startup chaos is a reality for many inexperienced founders. In many cases, the venture would not have failed if the founder had employed an integrated and methodical approach to building a company and not just a product.

The product-centric model sets no expectation of product completion.

Inherent in the current product-centric mindset is the attitude that one doesn't have to focus on completion. This is a problem because those who don't value completion miss out on joy and satisfaction of creating something and finishing it.

Second, it's bad business to build an incomplete product and hope investors will appear to help you finance the rest. It's like embarking on a long sea voyage with insufficient fuel and expecting to come across other ships that will help you re-fuel.

Third, this attitude is prevalent among founders who plan to build and flip their businesses as well as software-as-a-service founders. After all, if Gmail can be in Beta indefinitely, why not your own product?

Founders with a build-to-flip mindset aren't focused on product completion. They assume that by demonstrating proof of concept, they'll be able to raise additional money. But their approach to product development has no end goal. The "proof-of-concept" approach is a revolving door that goes nowhere.

They'd serve themselves better, if they didn't rush to demonstrate proof of concept until they covered all bases and spent time mastering presentation skills and preparing to answer investors' questions. Start-up pitches often consist of half-baked ideas and incomplete product demonstrations. In sum, for every startup that gets acquired by Yahoo or Facebook, there are untold unfinished products or services that are abandoned by founders.

Founder Insights

Focus on completion. You don't need a perfect product to showcase to potential investors, but you do need a complete product to demonstrate its viability. You do need to present a seamless user experience. And be prepared to roll out your seamless customer service.

The product-centric model reflects a sprinter's attitude, but a founder needs a marathoner's mindset.

Embedded in the current product-centric mindset is the expectation of speed—rapid development, execution, and delivery.

The upside: a company can sprint to achieve first-to-market, cutting-edge, and competitive status. The downside: getting to first place doesn't mean staying there. Speed doesn't guarantee enduring success. Speed can mean missed details and sloppy delivery. If you're cruising at 80 mph, you're sure to miss a few things you'd see at 25 mph.

Many first-time founders expend all their energies bringing what they believe is a unique product to the market. They exhaust themselves trying to demonstrate proof of concept: launch it quickly to get traction. Staying on course requires stamina, strength, and resources not anticipated and allocated. Pressure for speedy development distracts them from needs such as talent management, budget management, and resources management.

Founder Insights

Choose your speed and pace wisely. Know when you need to move quickly and when you need to expend proper time and energy—whether on team building, product development, marketing strategy, operations, brand development, or crisis response.

Don't rush—to showcase, to market, to respond—just because everyone else around you is rushing. Learn how to pace yourself so you don't run out of steam prematurely.

Take the long view. Adopt a marathoner's mindset. Build strength and endurance. Know what resources you will need on your long voyage; recognize it's not a day trip.

Anticipate that it will take longer than you think to achieve your goals and milestones—whether this means finding the right team member or supplier, raising money, setting up infrastructure, and/or establishing standards. Be prepared for delays and build in extra time to help you weather rough patches.

When too focused on building the product and proving its concept quickly, first-time founders ignore fundamental organizational principles and fail to build a proper foundation and infrastructure—all necessary to support a successful launch and growth.

Seasoned founders can have better success with the product-centric model because they know how to take the most efficient path while avoiding pitfalls.

Research All Financing Options Before You Begin

Today's founders have multitude of financial resources. Yet, very few research all options prior to embarking on their venture. Many first-timers set aside a startup budget to get the company going or prove their product idea. In their mind, they will research and figure out where the rest of the money comes from once they've started. Founders close to running out of money can stress out about a shutdown because cash flow hasn't turned positive.

To avoid this outcome, you need to research and study all the financing options available to new business owners. Read books on how to finance a new business. Find titles at your local library, your local bookstore, or online stores. Visit the SBA website for financing resources. Some local SBA offices also offer classes for entrepreneurs. Talk to local bankers, lenders, angel investors, and venture capitalists. Research their websites.

Learn about financing options before you embark—so that you have all of this information at your disposal and can incorporate that into your short-term as well as long-term plans. You don't want to wait until you need money and risk a shutdown.

You'll need to assess your financial habits and goals, too. And you'll need to address how you'll finance your venture. You'll practice these tasks in Chapters III, IV, and V.

Founder Insights

In the current startup environment, few founders self-finance their entire business (from startup through expansion phase) in order to have full control over it. Most founders find seed money to start their business and assume they'll need additional money to grow and expand. Consequently, they take on the burden of proving that their business is investment worthy. These founders handicap themselves with this assumption and mindset.

It is ironic that many pursue the entrepreneurial path because they're independent by nature; they want to realize their vision and run their own business. Yet they willingly give up control of their creation and become dependent on investors to enable them to complete product development and proceed to the next stage.

Most don't perform due diligence about their potential financiers and the investment landscape. Many serial entrepreneurs say they didn't know better the first time around, and gave up more equity and control than they should have.

In my years in the startup trenches, the successful were those whose founders self-financed. These founders were frugal. They boot-strapped. Most remain private to this day.

These founders didn't seek money because they were about to sink; they sought investors when they were profitable and ready to expand.

If you are building a new company so you can run your own business, research and reflect hard on how much of your company you are willing to give away in exchange for financing.

The more you give, the less control you have. What's the point in building a new company, if you end up working for your investors?

Decide for yourself when/if it's worth it. Once you've raised money to develop your product further and/or expand your business, be prudent with spending. I've worked for startups that spent their investors' money lavishly on office space and furniture, meals, latest technology, travel, and hotels. When they needed money for payroll, additional research, and product revisions, they had run out.

If you want to build and run your company, be self-reliant, not dependent. Avoid chasing after investors. Prove yourself and prove your product so that investors are chasing you. It is always better to be courted. Yet most first-time founders—in particular the build-to-flip ones—place themselves at the mercy of potential investors. Instead of creating and strengthening their position as sellers, most automatically assume it's a buyer's market.

The more you know about all your financing options, the more prepared you will be to negotiate with potential investors. Prepare well.

CHAPTER RECAP

Study the entrepreneurial scene before you embark.

- No formal training or certification is required to be a founder, but you must discover what qualifications and resources you possess and what you lack, if you are to refine and develop these prior to starting a new business.

- Learn from others' failures to avoid them.

- Distinguish false from legitimate startup information and insights.

- Recognize the Immediacy Mindset to make it work for you; avoid being held hostage. Organize your time, set boundaries, and manage expectations.

- Discover what you and your business need; avoid the herd.

- Assess the merits of the product-centric model to decide when and if it's appropriate for you. Prepare for your role as founder before you dive into product development.

- Research all financing options before starting your venture. Your research will be useful while you plan your financial strategy.

Now that you're familiar with the entrepreneurial landscape and understand the need to prepare well, let's focus on your development as founder.

Chapter II:
Employ a Framework to Develop as Founder

Your entrepreneurial journey is like a sea voyage with you as captain. As for a sea voyage, you'll want to be prepared for what you might face.

Plan Your Venture with an Integrated Mindset and Approach

Founder development starts with an integrated mindset. This means viewing every individual, entity, and process as something whole made of integral parts.[10]

As an individual, we each belong to one or multiple communities. As founder, you're an integral part of a team and so are your crew members. Your product is a critical part of your new business, which will require an infrastructure to launch, operate, and grow.

An integrated mindset holds that all essential components of an entity or an operation should synchronize harmoniously and organically. In reality, integration seldom occurs accordingly In particular, disorder is the norm within most startup operations So, it is especially helpful to employ this mindset so you'll always recognize how essential moving parts fit into the big picture of your life, your founder role, your operation, and your journey.

A new founder is more likely to succeed if s/he embark as an integrated individual; and a new business will have a higher chance of success if it's a well-integrated operation.

> *No man is an island, entire of itself.*
> *Every man is a piece of the continent, a part of the main.*
> John Donne

An Integrated Mindset

- The founder is an integrated individual
- The venture is an integrated entity

View the Founder as an Integrated Individual

As founder, you must determine what will be available for your venture. Begin with an understanding that we move through life each day with all that is in us: experiences, values, wisdom, instinct, habits, skills, dreams, goals, fears, successes, and failures. All of these affect decision-making. Each of us brings our whole self to each episode at home, play, or work. It's important to take stock of your life before starting a venture.

You'll need to integrate who you've been and what you've done with who you are and what you're doing. This will help you to know who you want to become and what you want to achieve. This includes identifying undeveloped parts of you that may be needed for future success. You'll want to strive for an integrated state where mind, spirit, heart, and body are in good to excellent shape and working in concert to support and nourish.

Develop and embark as an integrated individual and founder. Assess how your venture integrates into who you are. Begin a journey that will strengthen and affirm you. Advance your life path in a direction that feels right.

View the Venture as an Integrated Entity

Only a well-integrated engine will operate smoothly. A new venture requires time for planning, establishing standards, locating resources, acquiring talent, and setting a pace. You'll want to travel light, without unnecessary burdens. This means every material resource and every team member needs to fit well with your venture's purpose and core values.

Conversely, integration also occurs when the venture's purpose, values, brand identity, and standards permeate all aspects of your organization. This includes how you treat your employees and vendors, how you create and deliver your products, how your team communicates with your customers, how you obtain feedback, and how you build your company.

You'll want to think about how your business will integrate with your chosen industry. Will it align well with local and global markets, and the larger world? How will your product and entrepreneurial journey serve you, your family, and your community? How will the world be affected by your actions as founder? What positive or negative legacy are you creating?

Disruption has been the mindset for startups to embrace. Disruption can change outdated thinking and unhealthy habits. But not all disruption is good, especially disruption for its own sake. While your business idea may disrupt timeworn practices or monopolies, it can't exist in a disruptive mode; it needs stability of structure, standards, and processes. It needs to be an integrated operation that moves forward seamlessly.

Employ an integrated mindset and avoid building your operation piecemeal. Otherwise, you'll find yourself back at the drawing board trying to create infrastructure, systems, and processes for something that's partially constructed.

An Integrated Approach

An integrated approach takes account of what happens before you begin your venture. It includes the following important actions; these are listed sequentially. In reality, integration is not linear. Also, every individual is unique, so each may integrate differently.

Reflect

Reflect on your past. Bring clarity to your present and help prepare your future. Review what is yours: your intuition, wisdom, values, habits, winning approaches, successes, failures, challenges, powers, talents, skills, and life ambitions.

Assess

Evaluate all you uncovered during introspection. Decide what you want to jettison and what you're taking on your venture. Examine unresolved issues and questions newly emerged. Take note where you lack knowledge or competence.

Research

Research what you don't know. Prioritize issues and create an action plan to 1) refine or master needed skills, and 2) obtain resources you need to begin your venture.

Execute

Develop founder qualifications—whether by teaching yourself, taking classes, and/or working as an apprentice. Integrate what you've learned. Gather all you bring to your venture, which include all intangible and material resources. Create your manifest and move forward.

•••

An integrated mindset and approach will help you prepare well before starting out and keep you centered during your entrepreneurial journey so you won't lose sight of the big picture and the moving parts.

Understand Your Critical Role as Founder

As ship captain, you need to know what you're bringing on board in order to take the helm confidently. The most important thing you're bringing on board is you, not your product idea, which has no chance of success if you fail at the helm as skipper. The first step is to recognize and understand that you have the most critical role and shoulder immense responsibility.

- You're at the helm: you're in charge.
- You chart the course and set the pace.
- You have control over how you start your venture; the decisions you make before your trip can make or break it. You're responsible for everyone and everything you bring on board; gathering inadequate resources or choosing the wrong crew can affect your operation.
- You're responsible for strategic decisions that alter your future.
- When you encounter crises along the way, you're the one who resolves them.
- Your success depends on you.

The most common error that first-time founders make is failing to recognize the significance of their role and not preparing for it. Often, they're so excited with their product that they devote all their energy and resources to product development first. This is like taking command of a vessel without having studied seamanship.

A qualified captain possesses training and experience in ship handling, maritime law, cargo operations, celestial navigation, and crew operations. Train yourself so you will be well prepared.

Focus on Developing Competency

Start by assessing how qualified you are to assume the role of founder. If you lack skills, qualities, and training in certain areas, you'll need to develop basic competencies and hire those with needed skills and talents to support you. You don't need to be an expert in every function or role; you do need to acquire enough competence to ask the right questions for troubleshooting and problem resolution.

An important part of being competent is being self-reliant. When at sea, you have problems even when no other ship is in sight. Similarly, as you begin your venture, there will be crises, and no one will be available to help or else able to help because they aren't at the helm. You must be able to solve your own crises.

You won't have control over many factors in your venture, such as individuals or suppliers you hire, changes in markets, social or political currents, and emergence of new competitors or technologies. But you have control over you. You control what you know, what you're prepared to do, and what you're bringing aboard. You're the one who's always there for you. That's why self-reliance is essential.

Recognize Your Worth as Founder

Let's review the standard definition. Worth: usefulness or importance, as to the world, to a person, or for a purpose.[11]

Why is it important to know your worth? Knowing your worth helps you step forward from a position of strength. Everyone you want to enlist along the way—team members, strategic partners, investors, suppliers, and customers—will assess you as an individual and as founder. They'll assess your worth and your venture's worth. You need to know your worth and define it. If you don't define it, others will define it for you.

Many first-time founders rarely think about their worth. With a product-centric mindset, they assign high value to founding their company and creating a product with potential. They believe this should give them significant negotiating leverage and control of their venture. But this isn't enough. Founders must create value beyond having developed product and starting a company. Investors who find a founder lacking won't hesitate to replace her.

As an individual, your sense of worth is based on how you perceive a variety of things—your value as a unique human being, character and qualities, family heritage, life experiences, accomplishments and failures, bank accounts, possessions, connections, and contributions to your community and the world. Your sense of worth may be influenced by your perception of how others see and value you. Most important, your worth is based on how your value yourself.

As founder, your worth includes all these factors, and you bring them with you on your venture. But your worth is also determined by past and future performances. How well you execute during your initial startup phase and later will magnify or diminish your worth.

Founder Insights

Reflect on the following, as you focus on augmenting your worth:
- As an individual, what do you have that is priceless to you?
- As an individual, what tangible and intangible assets do you bring to your founder's role?
- As founder, what do you hold in your possession and what will you develop to augment your worth and your venture's worth during your entrepreneurial journey?

You must have a clear sense of your worth as an individual and as a founder—and not just in monetary terms.

Knowing your worth is essential, because:

- It empowers you to make decisions that serve and protect your interests and position.

- It gives you leverage when it comes to negotiating with new hires and new partnerships. You won't shortchange yourself with investors by giving away too much of your company for cash or other resources.

- It enables you to build on what you have (creating a product and starting a company) and magnify your worth (accomplishments in various roles beyond startup phase).

Focus on building your worth during your journey.

Envision Your Founder Role Throughout Your Venture's Life Cycle

Your venture a preparation, a start, a middle, and an end. As founder, you are the main and constant factor. Think about how you will fulfill your responsibilities and increase your worth as you move through each phase.

Preparation Phase

Everything you do or don't do before starting will have direct and profound effects on your venture. Reflect and define what a great start means to you.

- Research which tools, skills, and resources you need to acquire.

- Outline what you hope to accomplish during your Preparation Phase. Set goals and milestones for your venture.

Start Phase

Once you've started your voyage, you will know smooth sailing and rough waters. You'll need to overcome all kinds of challenges. You'll encounter developments over which you have no control. This include suppliers' price fluctuations to changing market trends; sudden resignation of a key team member; and new competitors. In addition to your founder role, you will need to perform other functional roles. What talents, skills, wisdom, and knowledge can you tap from within? Think about your various responsibilities and prepare yourself.

Growth Phase

As your venture gains momentum, you'll add team members. How will you evolve in your founder role? What additional functional roles will you assume? What new skills do you need to acquire? How can you increase your value, as you increase your contribution to the venture?

Exit Phase

If you decide to sell your business or step away, what skill sets do you need to help you position your company in an attractive light? How will buyers perceive your worth as founder? Will you be in such a strong position they'll court you for your business? Or will you get scant recognition and compensation for your role as founder?

Many first-timers fail to build their worth throughout their venture's life cycle. They focus only on their Start phase; they treat the Growth and Exit Phases as something far down the road. They don't plan ahead so they later find themselves unprepared and poorly positioned.

Monitor your own founder development and expanding responsibilities. Develop relevant skills to help you succeed. Build your worth and protect it as you progress.

Recognize the Importance of Your Own Manifest

Every captain needs a manifest. Your manifest is more than a document that lists cargo, passengers, and crew. It contains all your prep work and plans for your journey. It'll be your field guide, your Go-To resource, and your Survival Kit.

Your Field Guide

Your field guide comprises all the prep work that you will have done before starting your business: reflection, assessment, research, and organization. It will help you start your entrepreneurial journey, build your product and your team, and operate your business as an integrated enterprise.

You field guide will contain: 1) an overview of essential parts and 2) core elements that you can extract and incorporate into your business plan, which you may share with family, friends, new hires, partners, and investors.

Your Go-To Resource

The exercises that you will have performed will be your resource when you need affirmation for why you started this journey. You're full of enthusiasm starting out. You may not feel you need a boost now, but you will.

I've witnessed high and low moments in founders. As a serial founder myself, I've lived these highs and lows. Highs add fuel to momentum; lows can be debilitating and paralyzing. There'll be rough days in your entrepreneurial journey, days when you ask why you embarked in the first place, moments when you doubt your judgment and wonder whether you possess smarts, skills, talent, and perseverance to succeed.

You're fortunate if you have a network of family, friends, and mentors to provide you with emotional support and be cheerleaders. But they aren't living your founder's life; they can help only so far. Also, you'll experience crises when no one is around to call on, when everyone is occupied with their own priorities.

So, while you're feeling energized, enthusiastic, and grounded, you'll want to create your own support system—with yourself as your Number One fan. You will be your Go-To resource when you need to re-affirm faith in yourself and your venture.

Your Survival Kit

In today's round-the-clock connected world, many look outward for answers to problems. After all, "there's an app for everything." We rely on external sources to solve problems, whether internet searches, digital tools, crowd sourcing, and/or professional services. There'll be times when none of these will be accessible. When you're at sea and have no backup, what will you have to help you? What can you rely on to save yourself and your venture?

A founder needs to be as well qualified and prepared as can be. Since you can't plan for every crisis, you must be self-reliant.

The work that you do now, such as reflection, research, assessment, training, articulation, and organization—creating your manifest—will help you stock your Survival Kit so that you'll always be ready for emergencies and unanticipated disasters where help isn't available.

CHAPTER RECAP

Here's your framework for developing as a founder.

- Plan your venture with an integrated mindset and approach.

- Understand you have the most critical role and shoulder immense responsibility as founder.

- Recognize your need to develop competency before taking the helm.

- Acknowledge your worth as founder and focus on building it.

- Understand that each phase of your venture requires different skill sets. Take note of your expanding responsibilities and develop relevant skills for each phase to help you succeed.

- Monitor your founder development and protect your worth throughout your entrepreneurial journey.

Create your own manifest, which will prove essential on your journey as your field guide, your Go-To resource, and your Survival Kit. Your manifest will remind you why you undertook it—and how you're going to succeed.

Chapter III:
Invest in Yourself

Refine the self and set up the foundation.
Chang Po-Tuan (Translated by Thomas Cleary)

Once you begin, you'll be thinking, doing, and living your venture 24/7. It will require all you've got. You must be clear about all you bring to it.

When asked, "What do you bring to the table?" aspiring founders often point to their resumes and list operational expertise, industry experience, professional networks, and sometimes personal assets. When probed further, it becomes clear that most haven't thought much beyond these areas.

As founder, you bring more than just operational and industry experience. You bring your life's experiences with you wherever you go. Your instinct, wisdom, attitudes, values, habits, successes, failures, strengths, weaknesses, hopes, and fears influence your decision-making process every day. You will bring all this, all of you to your venture. All that you are will affect how you plan, execute, and respond to challenges. All that you are will determine how you interact with others, including under stress.

Before you move forward, take time for introspection and self-examination. Get updated on who you are. Be integrated in mind, body, heart, and spirit before taking on your new role. Failure to delve deeply in advance is frequent among first-time founders. Yet you need to understand what you, specifically, are bringing to your venture. First, take a snapshot of where you are today. Below are questions to get you started. Don't spend too much time on it. If you find yourself struggling to articulate an answer, leave the question unanswered for now and move on. When done, move to the next section. Return to unanswered questions later, after you've reflected on them.

Exercise 1: A Snapshot of Where You Are Today

1. Articulate what you love about your life.

Where You Are Today		
Area	What you love about your life	What you are doing to maintain or improve
Personal • Mind • Body • Spirit • Heart • Finance		
Home (Family)		
Work		
Community		

2. What is your center of gravity? Who or what grounds you as you move through daily life? Your grandmother, parents, best friend, children, partner, heritage?

3. What are your daily sources of stress? What are your recurrent challenges?

Recurrent Challenges		
Area	What are your daily sources of stress	How you manage or minimize them
Personal • Mind • Body • Spirit • Heart • Finance		
Home (Family)		
Work		
Community		

4. What are the three most important decisions you ever made?

Most Important Decisions		
Decision	Result: success or failure	Lesson learned
1.		
2.		
3.		

5. What are your lifelong aspirations? Are you living and working toward them? If not, what is hindering you, and what do you think is the cause? What can you do to get to closer to realizing your aspirations?

6. How do you envision living your life where everything is deeply aligned?

A Life Aligned		
Area	Ideal condition and situation	Actions you are taking to achieve it
Personal • Mind • Body • Spirit • Heart • Finance		
Home (Family)		
Work		
Community		

7. What are your priorities and goals for this year? For next year?

8. What are the top three reasons you want to leave your current situation?

9. Why do you want to start a new business? Before you answer this question, know that you might be having two conversations: 1) what you're telling the world, and 2) what you're telling yourself.

10. Why is your new business idea so compelling to you? Is this a must-do?

11. Why not work for an established company that offers a similar service or product?

12. How will your new entrepreneurial life align with your lifelong aspirations?

13. How do you think this new business will transform your life?

14. How will your product or service contribute to the world?

15. What are you willing to sacrifice to pursue this venture?

16. What will happen and how will you feel if you don't pursue it?

Make Time for Introspection

He that will not reflect is a ruined man.
Japanese proverb

The most important exercise that an aspiring founder can perform is introspection. It isn't the first thing that comes to mind for one who's excited about her product idea and contemplating a new venture. Yet it's crucial because while your business idea may evolve or change completely, the one constant that you want and need is a qualified and dependable skipper.

As founder, the one person whom you can rely on 24/7 is you. You want to be as competent, as well prepared as you can be. Start by allocating time to reflect and take stock of who you are, where you've been, where your life is, and what you're bringing on board to navigate your entrepreneurial voyage successfully.

Introspection is a gift you give yourself. If you're a reflective individual, then you have a head start. If you're one of those individuals who find it difficult to sit still, recognize that making time to be quiet and focus inward is a learned behavior. We can't hear our thoughts or feel our emotions, or become aware of our inner riches if we're distracted by round-the-clock news, to-dos, messaging apps, and crowds. If you can turn off your digital life for a few hours or a Saturday and be still, you'll see things you overlooked in your hurried pace. There is value in doing nothing, but you won't recognize it if you're in constant motion.

Introspection enhances self-awareness. In silence and stillness, reflect on your life and how they inform who you are. Articulate what all of you means and visualize how you want to evolve, what you want to accomplish. Introspection helps you understand why you make the decisions we do. It can prevent bad decisions as much as inform good decisions. It helps us know your strengths and areas you need to fortify. You'll start noticing blind spots and you'll become aware of habits that you've taken for granted; some have served you well and some you might want to jettison. Your personal riches will reveal themselves to you—if you give yourself time to uncover them.

In addition, introspection gives you a better understanding of others and the world around us. There is truth to the old adage that, "The answer lies within."

Yet, introspection isn't a priority because we juggle personal, familial, and professional demands, along with "maintenance tasks" of life in the 21st-century: fill the gas tank, pay bills, buy groceries, do laundry, and attend to children and parents. We scurry from one task or event to another. For most, life is a flurry of hurries.

For so many, we have no incentive to employ reflection as a tool for growth, solving problems, and clarifying what we think we know, want, and/or need. This is because we live bombarded by marketing messages that poke us on how we should live, what we should own, how to dress, what to eat, how to raise children, how and when to retire, and what drugs we'll need when we do. It's easy to avoid introspection, when answers can be found instantly online. And, "there's always an app for that."

We further undervalue introspection because being still and quiet makes us uncomfortable. We live in a society that encourages action and not repose. We don't make time for it, unless illness forces us to sit still or we hit a relationship crisis or a career roadblock. Even those who can afford time for thought find it challenging to be still and reflect deeply. For some, introspection is scary. It deals with issues we've long ignored. But if you have the courage to take the entrepreneurial path, you'll be able to tap that same courage to face issues thoughtfully.

Begin your introspection by reviewing and assessing several areas to articulate who you are and what makes you tick. This will help you integrate your past with your present and future.

- Identify Your Sources of Influence
- Assess Your Habits
- Review Your Accomplishments
- Analyze Your Failures
- Examine Your Window of Beliefs
- Uncover Your Sources of Power

Identify Your Sources of Influence

Start by identifying influences in your life. Most of us know what these are, but don't take time to articulate or probe them. We forget how much we're influenced by individuals, family, places, and past experiences, until forced by some crisis to turn inward for understanding and solutions.

Influencing sources may inspire or inhibit you. They color your values and prejudices; these will be reflected in your venture. They even affect your attitudes toward time management and human relations or how you spend money and resources. Your "sources of influence" affects your decision-making as a person and in your role as founder.

The more aware you are of what and who influences you, the more you'll understand why you act as you do, why you avoid certain things. And the more you understand, the more power and control you'll have over how you choose to respond to encounters on your journey.

Introspection will reveal insights and tools that you'll need. It includes blind spots and unexamined assumptions that you've held for a long time. Be courageous and open to what introspection reveals.

Exercise 2: Sources of Influence

Family

The adage "The apple doesn't fall far from the tree" is true. Our parents and relatives are our first sources of influence. Think about your family's history. Here are some questions that may help you reflect.

Identify Sources. What are family traditions or stories that have stayed with you? What are your grandparents' and parents' attitudes toward life, family, work, and play? Do they see life as a glass half full or half empty? What did they each prize the most? What standards or ideals did they try to uphold? What were their priorities?

Articulate. Think of three things that you've inherited from your family, which have shaped your beliefs, values, and daily conduct—negatively or positively. Who influenced you the most?

Family		
Tradition / Value / Habit / Attitude / Lesson learned	Positive or negative influence	How this source appears in your daily life
1.		
2.		
3.		

Friends

After parents, friends wield the most influence over many of us. We look to them for emotional support, as well as input on romantic interests, fashion choices, entertainment options, and career decisions.

Identify Sources. Which friends have influenced you the most?

Articulate. Think of three things that you've learned from friends, which have shaped your attitudes and behavior—negatively or positively.

Friends		
Tradition / Value / Habit / Attitude / Lesson learned	Positive or negative influence	How this source appears in your daily life
1.		
2.		
3.		

Role Models and Archetypes

Some have role models who aren't family or friends. Archetypes are personalities that appear in mythologies and folklores around the world. Archetypes include Hero, Warrior, Crusader, Explorer, Caregiver, Helper, Rebel, Revolutionary, Creator, Inventor, Scholar, Philosopher, Researcher, Thinker, Teacher, Builder, Catalyst, Visionary, and Leader. We encounter them in books, movies, and daily life. They lurk in our psyches and influence us.

For example, a schoolmate attended a talk by the Tibetan Buddhist Pema Chödrön and decided to become a monk. A friend—inspired by the medieval village's healer and herbalist—became a physician.

Identify Sources. What role models and archetypes influence and inspire you, other than family and friends? Why do they inspire you deeply?

Articulate. Think of three things that you've integrated into your daily life from your role models and archetypes.

Role Models and Archetypes		
Tradition / Value / Habit / Attitude / Lesson learned	Positive or negative influence	How this source appears in your daily life
1.		
2.		
3.		

School

We spent much of our growing years away from home in school.

Identify Sources. Who at school—teachers, coaches, counselors, and classmates—have left indelible marks on you?

Articulate. Think of three insights, approaches, or processes that you learned from those who taught and coached you. Include both healthy and unhealthy habits.

School		
Tradition / Value / Habit / Attitude / Lesson learned	Positive or negative influence	How this source appears in your daily life
1.		
2.		
3.		

Work

Work is where we spent much of our adult life. For many, work is a continuing education.

Identify Sources. What have you learned from your supervisors, peers, direct reports, vendors, and/or suppliers?

Articulate. Think of three insights, approaches, or processes that you picked up from your work life. Include healthy or unhealthy habits.

Work		
Tradition / Value / Habit / Attitude / Lesson learned	Positive or negative influence	How this source appears in your daily life
1.		
2.		
3.		

Environment
Our physical, cultural, and social environments affect our mental, emotional, and physical states. As you think about building a new environment, review how different environments affected you.

Identify Sources. Physical environments. Where did you grow up? Was it urban, suburban, or rural? Was it a wealthy or poor neighborhood? Was your family affluent or struggling? Did your family move around a lot or did you live in the same house until you went off to college?

Cultural/Social environments. Did you grow up in a religious, agnostic, or atheistic environment? Did you live in a homogeneous or multicultural neighborhood?

Articulate. Think about three insights you've culled from living, working, and interacting in different environments. How have they influenced your personal and professional decisions?

Environment		
Tradition / Value / Habit / Attitude / Lesson learned	Positive or negative influence	How this source appears in your daily life
1.		
2.		
3.		

Now that you've thought about various sources of influence, over the next few weeks, think about how they may affect you as founder.

Assess Your Habits

We each carry a lifetime of acquired habits—from our parents, friends, teachers, colleagues, partners, and peers. Some were acquired by choice or fancy; others by necessity—for work, health reasons, or survival.

We wake up each day to navigate through a routine that includes home, family, work, and community. Punctuality, responsiveness, and resourcefulness are some "habitual tools" we employ to move through each day. Mostly, we don't give much thought to these tools because they're second nature. We become aware of them when a mishap occurs, or when someone points them out.

As founder, be aware of your habits, which will give you insight into habits of others. Reinforce good ones and bring them on board; jettison bad ones. Assess your habits.

- General Habits
- Mental Habits
- Work Habits
- Financial Habits
- Wellness Habits

General Habits

Most of us rely heavily on daily habits without taking time to assess them. Evaluate the following eight habits.

Exercise 3: General Habits

General Habits	
Habit	Rate where you are with each habit (1 = abysmal; 2 = competent; 3 = strong; 4 = excellent). Decide an action for growth if you see room for improvement
1. Punctuality (Strict observance in keeping engagements; promptness)	
2. Responsiveness (The act of responding readily to appeals, efforts, influences, etc.)	
3. Responsibility (The state of being answerable or accountable for something within one's power, control, or management)	
4. Diligence (Constant and earnest effort to accomplish what is under taken)	
5. Trustworthiness (The state of deserving of trust or confidence; dependability; reliability)	
6. Collaboration (Working with others)	

General Habits	
Habit	Rate where you are with each habit (1 = abysmal; 2 = competent; 3 = strong; 4 = excellent). Decide an action for growth if you see room for improvement
7. Resourcefulness (Ability to deal skillfully and promptly with new situations, difficulties; problem solving)	
8. Integrity (Adherence to moral and ethical principles; honesty)	

Mental Habits

Understanding how you learn helps you be more aware of where you're strong and what you need to strengthen. It also helps you be more aware of how others learn. This will ultimately help you become a better founder-captain, manager, student, mentor, and collaborator.

Exercise 4: Method of Learning

How You Learn		
Method	Rank them in the order of most preferred (1) to least preferred (5) method	Assess and note what works well for you and where you want to improve
1. Reading		
2. Listening		
3. Watching a tutorial, a demonstration, or observing a behavior		

How You Learn		
Method	Rank them in the order of most preferred (1) to least preferred (5) method	Assess and note what works well for you and where you want to improve
4. Discussing with others; collaborating		
5. Doing or testing (trial and error)		

Exercise 5: Time of Day You Learn Best

Some absorb new information or techniques in the morning. Others don't become alert until the evening. When is the best time for you to learn? If you haven't paid attention to this, you'll want to develop awareness of it to improve your learning habits. Knowing when you best learn or study can help you plan time more effectively.

When You Learn Best	
Time of day	Rank your most effective (1) to least effective time period (7)
Early morning	
Late morning	
Noon time	
Early afternoon	
Early evening	
Late evening	
After midnight	

Exercise 6: Settings Where You Learn Most Effectively

Ideal Condition for Learning	
Setting	Rank your most effective (1) to least effective setting (5)
1. By yourself, in silence	
2. By yourself, with background music or noise	
3. In group setting (classroom, workshops, library, or coffee shop)	
4. In a corporate setting (open floor plan, cubicle, or private office)	
5. Other	

If you're going from an office job with many colleagues to your own home office, how will you adjust to this change? What environment and conditions will you create?

Exercise 7: Thinking Habits

We rely on our minds to work for us without taking the time to reflect on how we process information, observations, and insights. How we think affects how we act, decide, or refrain from deciding. Review what you take for granted each day.

How do you think? Examine your thinking style and enhance your awareness of how others think. Below are descriptions of different types of thinkers. These are a few profiles to help you reflect on your thinking process. No one is a "purist" thinker. You may find yourself possessing a combination of thinking styles, with some more dominant than others.

How You Think	
Profile and Characteristics	Rate yourself (1 = least like me; 2 = somewhat; 3 = strongly; 4 = most like me)
1. The realist / pragmatist • Recognizes the constraints and uses what is available. • Blind spot: may be too pragmatic and less willing to consider creative or unconventional solutions.	
2. The idealist • Strives for higher standards and ideals. • Blind spot: may wait for ideal conditions and ignore problems that need to be resolved immediately.	
3. The strategist • Approaches the journey or problem with a big picture and long-term perspective. • Blind spot: may miss the finer details and immediate issues that need attention and resolution.	
4. The tactician • Focuses on solving current challenges; executes with precision and thoroughness. • Blind spot: may miss the view of the big picture.	

How You Think	
Profile and Characteristics	Rate yourself (1 = least like me; 2 = somewhat; 3 = strongly; 4 = most like me)
5. The eclectic • Is open to all kinds of ideas, perspectives, and resources; solves problems with a unique / unconventional approach. • Blind spot: may juggle too many factors and lack focus.	
6. The purist • Makes decisions based on what s/he was taught as effective; doesn't deviate from time-honored practices. • Blind spot: may be too rigid when problem solving requires flexibility and compromise.	

Knowing about the different styles of thinking can help you refine your own style and become more aware of how future employees, business partners, and suppliers think, and if their styles align or conflict with yours. Note that you don't want those around you to all have the same style as you; diversity is a plus to discerning emerging problems.

In addition to this exercise, read books on thinking styles to develop deeper self-awareness.

Exercise 8: Decision-making Habits

We make small to big decisions every day. Our backgrounds, genetic talents, skills, and personal wisdom shape our decision-making habits.

As a founder, you'll be on the spot for strategic and tactical decisions. Understand how you make decisions, and note how those around you make decisions. When you understand and trust the decision-making process of employees and colleagues, you can delegate easily. You communicate and negotiate with more clarity and efficiency. For a week or two, observe how you make decisions.

Situation 1: When it comes to what to wear, what to eat, what daily tasks to prioritize, how do you describe your decision-making habit?

Situation 2: When it comes to big decisions like where to attend university, what career path to pursue, when to change jobs, when to make a big purchase or who to marry, how do you describe your decision-making habit?

Situation 3: Think of personal, familial, and professional crises you have encountered, where your decision was needed. How do you describe your decision-making habit?

How You Decide	
Profile and characteristics	Rate yourself (1 = least like me; 2 = somewhat; 3 = strongly; 4 = most like me)
Decisive • You review only information that is available to you. You conduct no additional research, consider the pros and cons, and decide quickly. • Blind spot: not recognizing that some decisions require waiting for additional information and deliberation.	

How You Decide	
Profile and characteristics	Rate yourself (1 = least like me; 2 = somewhat; 3 = strongly; 4 = most like me)
Thoughtful and measured • You research extensively all options, consider the pros and cons, and then decide. You cannot be pressed into a hurried decision. • Blind spot: not recognizing that sometimes you cannot afford the time for in-depth research.	
Procrastinating • You avoid researching and making decisions until the last minute. • Blind spot: lack of research and attention to time-sensitive issues can lead to loss of opportunity, crisis or failure.	

Clearly, different situations call for different decision-making processes. Assess and decide where you need to refine.

In addition to this exercise, read books on decision-making styles and cognitive biases to develop deeper self-awareness.

Work Habits

As founder, you create a working environment most suitable to you. It's important to understand how you work so you can optimize time and resources. You'll need to understand each new team member's work style, and how that fits into your venture. This will help you identify opportunities for synergy. New companies often run into glitches because founders didn't set up working criteria for team members to observe. When there are no definitions, standards, and processes in place, chaos occurs. When people don't know what's expected, miscommunication occurs.

Most of us adapt to corporate structures of our jobs. We took them for granted and have not reflected on our own working standards, rhythms, productivity patterns, and preferred environments. Now is a good time to assess how you work.

Exercise 9: Work Standards
On the personal and professional levels, we hold ourselves to certain ethical, moral, and performance standards. To one individual, this means punctuality. To another, it means dedicated workspace and an organized schedule. To another, it means exceeding expectations and always delivering a bit more to clients than promised. Review and assess.

Work Standards	
What daily work standards and habits do you have in place for yourself? Articulate three that have served you well.	
What are your recurrent challenges? What's the one task that can help you improve?	
New practice(s) that you would like to add in your founder role.	

Exercise 10: Work Rhythm
Most of us must live by a corporate working schedule of 8-to-6. Yet most of us have never taken time to discover if this routine suits us; some aren't aware of circadian rhythms, their working rhythm, or productivity pattern.

Alan Lakein, an expert on personal time management, wrote about Prime Time in his book, *How to Get Control of Your Time and Your Life*.[12] Internal Time is when you work best—morning, afternoon, or evening. External Prime Time is the best time to attend to other people—those you have to deal with in your job, intramural sports, volunteer work, and so on. Review and assess.

Work Rhythm	
What are your internal and external prime times? Are you a night owl or a morning person?	
How would you describe natural working rhythm? For example: work straight for hours without break, or work with needed breaks.	
If you are aware of your internal and external prime times, how have you made them work for you?	
What are your recurrent challenges? What's one task that can help you optimize your work rhythm?	

Exercise 11: Productivity Pattern

You may know about the 80/20 rule. The Italian economist Vilfredo Pareto came up with this formula, which holds true across many disciplines and industries: 80% of results come from 20% of efforts; 80% of sales come from 20% of products; 80% of revenues come from the top 20% customers.[13] Review and assess.

Productivity Pattern	
Think about your life at home and at work. What are key drivers that affect your daily productivity level?	
How would you describe your daily productivity level? Are you an 80/20? A 50/50, a 70/30, or a 90/10?	
What is your optimal productivity ratio and are you achieving it frequently / steadily?	
Implement one or two tasks to improve your productivity level.	

Exercise 12: Work Environment

As founder, you get to create your work environment. Review all your prior work environments as well as the work you did under Work Habits section. Take note of what has worked well for you and what needs to change.

Work Environment	
Are you most productive working in a closed-door office or in an open-floor plan?	
Do you need white noise or background noise in order to be productive?	
Do you work best alone or around people?	
What is your ideal work environment?	

Think about your preferred work habits and changes you can make to improve them. List all your criteria and prioritize your must-haves.

Financial Habits

Before starting your venture, review and assess your attitudes toward money and how these affect your financial habits. You want to leverage strengths and identify habits you may need to monitor or improve.

Exercise 13: Financial Habits

Ask yourself the questions below. Reflect carefully about your financial habits, and project how you will spend and save as a founder.

1. Describe your attitude toward money. Do you view it as a positive resource or a stressful necessity?

2. Do you love numbers? Are you good with accounting? Or do you avoid dealing with numbers?

3. Is money something that comes easily for you or do you worry about it all the time?

4. Do you enjoy making money? Spending it? Saving it? Hoarding it?

5. Are you known as someone who is parsimonious, frugal, cautious, or spendthrift?

6. Where does the money you make go?
   - Personal (appearance, fitness, recreation) _____
   - Family / Home _____
   - Work _____
   - Savings _____
   - Other _____

7. How would you describe your financial habits?
   • Dismal and needing an overhaul _____
   • Juggling with room for improvement _____
   • Sensible with occasional indulgences _____
   • Disciplined _____

8. What positive habits should you keep and which ones should you monitor, improve, or jettison?

Startup Anecdotes

Many first-time entrepreneurs don't give much thought to financial habits before starting ventures. One corporate lawyer-turned-entrepreneur spent like he was still working in his swanky law firm, when he should have been bootstrapping.

I worked with a few founders who were careless when it came to investors' money; they wrongly believed that because they'd been successful in raising money the first round, there was more to come. Consequently, they didn't budget or bootstrap. They went on a hiring binge and splurged on office space and equipment. Before acquiring enough paying customers to cover overhead costs, they ran out of money and had to shut down.

Other founders were so tight with money that while they expected best service and performance from others, they weren't willing to pay for it.

If you're someone who spends liberally, monitor your habit and be cautious with your startup's budget. If you're someone who count pennies, beware that cutting corners at the start may create operational problems later. For example, not paying people what they're worth led to resentment, poor performance, and high turnover.

Your attitude toward money and your financial habits can help build your venture, or lead to a shutdown.

Wellness Habits

Starting a company is exciting; it's also stressful. I've known founders who were in excellent health when they started out. Within a year, they gained weight, suffered insomnia, and developed high blood pressure. One founder's dormant asthma reappeared; another developed digestive issues. They claimed they didn't have time to exercise.

Exercise 14: Wellness Habits

Wellness Habits		
Area	Rate your wellness status (1 = poor; 2 = average; 3 = good; 4 = excellent). What helps you stay fit	Action that is needed to maintain or improve your wellness status
Mind		
Body		
Spirit		
Heart		

As I've mentioned before, you need to assume that your journey is a marathon instead of a sprint. Your wellness is important because you need strength and endurance. You need to be in good to excellent health. This means eating right, getting enough sleep, exercising, making time to clear your mind and spirit, and resolving emotional conflicts. You need to decompress from daily stress and recharge. If you don't, you will find yourself beset with physical and mental health issues. This, in turn, will affect your performance as founder and your startup's well-being.

Review Your Accomplishments

Think about how your accomplishments and lessons learned may influence you in your founder role.

Exercise 15: Best Decisions

Review the best decisions you've made in life, such as deciding where to attend college, when to take your first solo adventure, skill sets you decided to learn, first internship you took, whom you married, and where you chose to live. A great decision can mean deciding against something—not to move, not to take a job, and so on.

Best Decisions			
Decision	Situation / Condition	Instinct / Skill / Talent / Tool you employed	How decision affected your life
1.			
2.			
3.			

Exercise 16: Best Form

Think about the times when you were at the top of your game. What factors or qualities enabled you to be in top form?

Best Form			
Instant when you were at top of your game	Situation / Condition	Instinct / Skill / Talent / Tool you employed	How each affected your life
1.			
2.			
3.			

Exercise 17: Winning Approach

Some individuals have developed a tried-and-true formula for accomplishing a fitness goal, a financial goal, or a career goal. Do you have a winning approach? What are your recurrent successes?

Winning Approach			
Action / Pattern of success	Situation / Condition	Instinct / Skill / Talent / Tool you employed	How this affected your life
1.			
2.			
3.			

Exercise 18: Challenges Overcome

Think about the most difficult challenges that you have encountered and how you overcame them successfully.

Challenges Overcome			
Challenge resolved successfully	Situation / Condition	Instinct / Skill / Talent / Tool you employed	How this affected your life
1.			
2.			
3.			

Analyze Your Failures

Exercise 19: Worst Decisions

We've all made huge blunders at one time or another. Own and analyze your missteps so you will remember what to avoid, what to monitor.

Worst Decisions			
Biggest blunder you've committed	Situation / Condition	Instinct / Skill / Talent / Tool you should have employed	How this affected your life
1.			
2.			
3.			

Exercise 20: Recurrent Challenges

We all have issues that we struggle with time and again. These may include not listening well, not taking a stand, avoiding confrontation, overcommitting, always running late, or overspending. As you're taking stock of your tools for your venture, acknowledge these challenges and address them.

Recurrent Challenges			
Recurrent challenge	Recurrent pattern of response	How this has affected your life	Skill / Talent / Tool / Action / Attitude that may resolve
1.			
2.			
3.			

Exercise 21: Hot Buttons

We all possess sensitive areas where an event or a comment may trigger the nasty beast within. Acknowledge your hot button issues. Learn how to self-manage so you can minimize or avoid situations that may trigger them.

Hot Buttons			
Issue	Recurrent pattern of response	How this has affected your life	Skill / Talent / Tool / Action / Attitude that may resolve
1.			
2.			
3.			

Examine Your Window of Beliefs

We each view the world through a unique window of beliefs about life, time, money, family, friends, and work. This is the result of experiences and various sources of influence. Our beliefs affect attitudes, which affect our actions. Next is an exercise to help you examine your beliefs.

Example: Sam's Window of Beliefs and How It Rules Sam	
Belief	Action reflecting belief
• I am an optimist. I see life as a glass half full. I view life as a journey with ups and downs, twists and turns.	• I always choose to focus on the upside and solve problems from this perspective.
• I believe everyone has something to contribute.	• I try to consider an individual's opinion or position before rejecting or accepting it.
• I value Time and see it as a resource, not as an adversary.	• I am always punctual because I respect my time and show others I respect theirs.

When you have insight into your own beliefs, you'll have insight into how others see the world and why they act as they do. You'll become aware of those who share similar beliefs and those who differ from you.

Exercise 22: Window of Beliefs

How Your Beliefs Rule You	
Belief about life	Action reflecting belief
Belief about self	Action reflecting belief
Belief about family	Action reflecting belief
Belief about work	Action reflecting belief
Belief about play	Action reflecting belief
Belief about time	Action reflecting belief
Belief about money	Action reflecting belief
Belief about people	Action reflecting belief

In the next few weeks, give yourself time to think about how your beliefs will affect your actions as founder.

Uncover Your Sources of Power

> *The most common way people give up their power*
> *is by thinking they don't have any.*
> Alice Walker

Each day, we wield all kinds of power, but seldom analyze it. Before starting your venture, reflect on what powers you possess so you know what you can access.

The standard definition for power is the ability to do or act.[14] This includes acting physically, mentally, emotionally, legally, morally, financially, technically, and artistically. Power that you exert over yourself can be thought of as agency, self-management, self-discipline, or self-mastery. Power that you exert over others may be viewed as clout—ability to influence someone's thinking and actions.

Do you know your sources of power? How well do you wield them? Here's one way of viewing and uncovering your powers.

Internal Sources of Power

Your internal sources of power are those that you access from within, any time, anywhere. They are available in the following realms:

- Mental – Analytical, technical, intellectual, problem solving skills, and curiosity.
- Spiritual – Faith in whatever inspires, grounds, and nurtures you.
- Emotional – Ability to manage your emotions, connect with and relate to others, express, and exercise restraint when appropriate.
- Physical – How you appear, present yourself, and communicate.

You also have your intuition and wisdom at your disposal. We often take these qualities for granted and don't give much weight to them as sources of power. Most of us don't even acknowledge to ourselves that we possess wisdom; it's not in vogue in today's culture, which fixates on power that's tangible and measurable.

You can access your mental faculties, emotional temperament, spiritual foundation, and physical well-being at any time. Cultivate them. Nurture them so they can serve you at any moment.

External Sources of Power

Your external sources of power may include:

- Reputation / personal brand
- Money
- Assets – Material possessions, intellectual property, etc.
- Position – Your standing within your company, your industry niche, your community, and organizations where you are a formal or informal member.

External sources of power can enhance personal clout and expand spheres of influence. But you may not always have access to external sources of power. Use them to prepare and build your business, but tap what is accessible to you 24/7.

Startup Anecdotes

An engineer founded a company and assumed three positions: founder, CTO, and CEO. Ken was insecure about his CEO responsibilities and powers from the start. He was most comfortable with technical skills so he often hid in his CTO office. He surfaced to deal with team management, business development, and operations—when pressed for a decision as Founder-CEO.

His startup moved along, but never took off at full steam because Ken was seldom at the helm. After four years, tired of his CEO duties, Ken sold his business to a competitor who shut it down.

•••

An individual named Jess and her spouse bankrolled a new business. They both took the title "Co-Founder" and decided that Jess would assume the CEO position during early years. Jess struggled as CEO because she found the accompanying powers and responsibilities overwhelming. While Jess excelled at product and market research, she acknowledged that she chafed when she had to exercise her CEO powers, like firing incompetent engineers, developing new clients, and negotiating new deals. This reluctance led her to neglect one of her main duties, which was to lead her team members during a critical time that required her presence. Because she wasn't at the helm, her crew deserted, and the venture stalled.

Many first-time founders assume the CEO role without spending time researching and reflecting on what it means to wear the CEO hat—perform required duties and wield accompanying powers. Many assume this role completely unprepared. This is a common blind spot and an understandable one.

Founder Insights

On a daily basis, most of us don't spend time thinking about our powers. Instead we give them away because we're taught to look outward for power, money, possessions, and status. We endow holders of these with power.

We're not taught to recognize innate resources that we can develop and use to magnify our power. Knowing what your internal powers are and when to tap them empowers. When self-aware and self-possessed, you invoke recognition for your internal powers.

You have the power:
- To say, "Yes," but only when you are ready and confident with your decision.
- To say, "No" to an offer that doesn't work for you.
- Not to shortchange yourself or undervalue your business.
- To ask for more—because you believe in what you're offering.

As a self-reliant and prepared founder, you'll need all your powers.

Exercise 23: Sources of Power

Internal Sources of Power		
Internal power	How and when do you wield this power	How do you rate this power? (1 = weak, 2 = competent, 3 = strong, 4 = excellent / second nature)
Mental		
Spiritual		
Emotional		
Physical		

External Sources of Power		
External power	How and when do you wield this power	How do you rate this power? (1 = weak; 2 competent; 3 = strong; 4 = excellent / second nature)
Reputation / Personal brand		
Money		
Assets		
Position (social, professional, and community)		

Reflect on all your powers. How often do you tap them? Which have served you well? Which do you want to strengthen? Think about how you will carry your powers into your venture, and how you will deploy and exercise them.

From Introspection to Integration

Now that you've spent time reflecting and assessing, you should have a better understanding of how you allocate time, where you're most effective, and where you need to improve. You should have more clarity regarding how your past has influenced you, where and who you are in your present, and what you can take with you on your venture.

Your Introspection time should give you more clarity regarding the following issues; these should be articulated and addressed before stepping into your new role. Don't stress if you don't have an immediate answer; sometimes it takes a while before an answer appears.

State Your Purpose

Exercise 24: Purpose

1. What is your life's purpose? How is your purpose reflected in your daily life, in your personal life, and in your work life?

2. What are your current life's priorities? What are your daily and weekly priorities? Do they reflect your purpose? What action plan do you have in place to ensure you are achieving your purpose and honoring those priorities?

3. What have you accomplished? Are you meeting your short-term and long-term goals? What else do you want to realize?

4. What is your personal brand? If someone had to describe your brand, what would you like to hear her say? What do you do to build it, maintain it, and refine it?

5. What kind of legacy do you want to create?

Articulate Your Core Values

Exercise 25: Core Values

What are your core values? How are they present in your personal as well as professional life?

Core Values	
Value	Daily action that reflects value
1.	
2.	
3.	

Know Your Main Influencers

Now that you've spent time examining your past and reacquainting yourself with sources of influence, prioritize the top three that affect your daily outlook and inform your decision-making. It's important to know who and what inspires or what hinders you, because this will influence your actions as founder.

Exercise 26: Main Influencers

Top Sources of Influence	
Sources of influence that affects you positively	Sources of influence that you need to jettison
1.	
2.	
3.	

Acknowledge What Drives You

Exercise 27: Motivation

1. What drives you to take action, to accomplish all that you have thus far in your life?

2. What compels you to embark on this entrepreneurial path? This is the first question I often ask of new founders.

You may be having two conversations. The first is what you're telling the world about why you're starting a new business, and the second is what you're telling yourself.

Give yourself time to mull over the questions. Write down the answer. Look at it often. Revise. If you find yourself struggling for an answer, you need to dig deeper. Revise until you have a concise answer that reflects your true motivation. If you can't find your true conviction, you may find yourself faltering during crises.

Here are answers given by past founders:
- "Realize my dream of running my own business by leveraging my passion and talents."
- "Work for myself and not for a corporation."
- "Obtain more flexibility in my work routine for family reasons."
- "Have more creative freedom."
- "Obtain financial independence."
- "Create a new service or a new product because a family member needs it, and there's no such product in the market."

Note Your Habits

Previously, you've spent some time reviewing and assessing various habits. Prioritize the top three that serve you well and those that you need to monitor or let go.

Exercise 28: Habits

Habits	
Habit you that serve you well	Habit that you need to monitor or jettison
1.	
2.	
3.	

Evaluate Your Work-in-Progress

Introspection should have shed some light into areas in need of improvement: your work-in-progress. Before you begin a new chapter, articulate those you need to address.

Exercise 29: Work-in-Progress

Work-in-Progress	
Area	Issue to address and how they may affect your founder role
Personal • Mind • Body • Spirit • Heart • Finance	
Home (Family)	
Work	
Community	

Think about how they may affect your founder role.

Adopt a Wholistic, Integrated Mindset

Seasoned founders will tell you that an entrepreneur's life can be all-consuming. So how do you prepare for it and keep it in perspective?

Envision living your life in a "wholistic" manner. View work as one component of your integrated life; think about how you will incorporate your entrepreneurial life into it.

Exercise 30: An Integrated Life

A Wholistic, Integrated Life		
Area	Ideal condition and goal	Action you're taking to achieve it
Personal • Mind • Body		
• Spirit • Heart • Finance		
Home (Family)		
Work		
Community		

CHAPTER RECAP

In this chapter, you spent much time in reflection and assessment.

- You've identified your sources of influence. You have an updated understanding of how they've inspired or inhibited you, how they've affected your attitudes and your decision-making process.

- You've assessed your habits and taken note of effective ones as well as recurrent challenges.

- You've reviewed best decisions, accomplishments, and winning approaches. You've analyzed worst decisions, failures, and hot buttons. You've taken note of lessons learned.

- You've examined your window of beliefs, and understood how it influences your decision-making process.

- You've uncovered your internal and external sources of power. You know what you can access on your journey.

- You've affirmed your purpose and core values, and you've identified what/who grounds you and motivates you.

- You've evaluated your work-in-progress and have thought about how they may affect you in your founder role.

- You've recognized how a "wholistic" mindset can help you: 1) shift your present life into a strong and healthy position, 2) start your entrepreneurial life prepared, and 3) manage your entrepreneurial life so you don't lose perspective of the big picture.

Now that you've gone from introspection to assessment to articulation, you are more self-aware and self-engaged than before, and more integrated as you approach the next chapter: preparing for your role as a founder.

Chapter IV:
Develop Founder Competency

Beginning is easy, continuing is hard.
Japanese Proverb

Your manifest has two parts: the first focuses on you: the founder. Think of it as your captain's chest of tools and resources. It's what you're bringing on board to start your venture, keep it going, and keep it focused. It will support you when crises arise.

Most first-time founders who take the helm scarcely think about essential qualities that they—as captain of their entrepreneurial journey—should possess. Most are focused on developing their product idea. Many don't question their qualifications until they hit rough seas. Then they discover they lack qualities or skills needed to survive. Avoid this most common oversight. Ensure that you'll begin with confidence and competence. What do you need to do to be ready?

Keep in Mind the Big Picture

Whether you're building a company of 10 or 1,000, you need to think about what kind of founder you will be. What functional roles will you perform throughout the venture's life cycle? Below are the main roles of a business entity. Titles vary depending on industry, but they're essentially the same. Keep this structure in mind as you research, assess, define, and develop your founder role.

Basic Organization - Top Level Structure

Founder
Is idea originator, visionary, cheerleader, product developer, launcher, builder, business developer, fund-raiser, and operator.

Chief Executive Office (CEO)
Is in charge of total management of a corporate entity. Main duties include: leader, crisis manager, decision maker, communicator, cheerleader, and fund-raiser.

President
• Works closely with vice president, chief financial officer, and chief operating officer to implement the company's strategic plan.
• Modifies the company's strategy according to company needs, market trends, and economic conditions.
• Presides over the organization's day-to-day operations.

Chief Financial Officer (CFO)
Is responsible for financial planning and record keeping, and the company's financial health.

Chief Marketing Officer (CMO) / Vice President Marketing
Oversees research, product, communications, strategic planning, and customer service.

Chief of Technology (CTO) / Vice President Engineering
Is responsible for technological-related decisions and policy, which may include scientific research, company security, and customer privacy. In some cases, the CTO is also responsible for product strategy.

Vice President of Business Development
Oversees new business acquisitions, new market entries, and sales strategies.

Counsel
Ensures the business is compliant on various legal fronts: business filings, intellectual properties, labor law, environmental compliance, product compliance, and contract negotiations.

Recognize, Assess, and Plan Involvement Through the Venture

Your business will have four phases: preparation, start, growth, and exit. The following tasks may fall within these phases, depending on each business' unique needs, goals, and development pace. Review what needs to be accomplished and plan your involvement.

Four Phases

Preparation Phase
Founder development and preparation

Start Phase
- Ideation, research, and development
- Business formation, structure, standards, and processes
- Market research, customer profiling
- Concept refinement, prototype / product development, and launch

- Brand positioning, marketing, and business development
- Sales channel development
- Team building and talent management
- Operational expansion

Growth Phase
- Customer segmentation development
- New market research, prototypes, and product launches
- New sales channel development
- Team expansion
- Operational expansion

Exit Phase
Factors that may lead to your decision to exit
- You've achieved financial goals and want to sell
- You're bored and you want to sell
- Your market segment is saturated; consumption level remains flat
- Consumer demand is declining due to changing tastes
Preparation for sale / shut down

Think about how you will augment your founder's worth during various phases:

- Your founder role before your start,
- Your role(s) when you start,
- Your role(s) after you've started your venture (how you plan to develop it, strengthen it) and,
- Where you may be on your voyage when you want to fold your business.

Now that you have the big picture in mind, focus on your founder role first; and recognize that you need to serve as a role model who embodies standards that you want your crew to observe.

Develop Founder Competency

Earlier I pointed out that no training or certification is required to practice as an entrepreneur. Many first-time founders and co-founders put their best foot forward, but didn't know what they didn't know, unlike a trained physician or accountant. Because founders stumble, they need help preparing for their roles.

As a founder, you'll need what I call Founder Competency. This is a set of essential skills and qualities that enable you to take the helm and navigate through your journey. They're also an integral part of your founder's worth.

Most likely, you've already mastered some in a former or current job. Focus on those you need to strengthen. If you avoid those that make you uncomfortable, you'll weaken yourself. You may even lead your venture to crisis, if not failure. Review these skills and qualities; commit to developing competency before starting your venture.

Founder Competency
- Core action skills
- Core management skills
- Core qualities
- Financial preparedness
- Industry experience
- Survival skills

We begin with five core action skills required for your founder role.

The Founder's Core Action Skills
1. Initiate
2. Plan
3. Execute
4. Solve
5. Lead

Initiate

Personal initiative is the heart of starting and growing a new business, especially after the initial high at the launch. You'll need it to create opportunities, find customers and collaborators, and solve problems. You'll experience stops and starts, and that's when personal initiative is essential.

Founder Insights

Many founders are good at taking the initiative, but they are not so great at following through. Make sure you follow through.

The flip side of taking the initiative is knowing how to wait for an answer, wait for a development. Keeping options open may be the best strategy.

Plan

According to time management expert Alan Lakein, "We bring the future to the present by planning." Planning is actually more about strategic thinking than strategic planning. You can "plan" by making sure you possess the appropriate qualifications for your venture, and by gathering the tools and resources to help you solve whatever challenges may arise. You can create a road map, but given today's fast changing business conditions, make that Version 1.

Founder Insights

Sometimes, even though you thought you had prepared well, you realize that you are ill-equipped for a new situation. In this case, you "plan" by being ready to improvise, make do with what is available, and resolve that situation.

Execute

As founder, you need to implement your plans and accomplish your goals. You need to take action and move your venture forward.

Founder Insights

Impatient and overly confident founders rush ahead and execute without research or reflection. Insecure founders become paralyzed by fear and wait for someone else to make decisions. Knowing the right time to execute is important.

Solve

As founder, you are responsible for solving all issues that come your way, until you have a team to support you and you can delegate.

Founder Insights

Knowing your process for solving problems is essential. Recognizing how others solve problems helps you determine what is appropriate for your venture—from an immediate as well as long term perspective.

Lead

As a founder, you wear the leadership hat. You create the vision. You lead and inspire your team, keep them focused, and help them deliver. You must appear as a leader to all your collaborators, from investors to vendors, to ensure their support of your vision.

Some are born leaders. Even if you're a natural, there's room for growth. Others chafe at the thought of leading. If you recognize this in yourself, start developing your leadership skill now. Don't avoid it.

Founder Insights

A good leader is one who is accessible to your team, one whose presence provides stability and inspiration.

A true leader also knows when to lead and when to follow.

You don't discover what kind of leader you are until you're doing it. So, give yourself some room for learning and growing.

Evaluate Your Founder's Core Action Skills

Clarify your attitude. When you think of each of the following skills, what emotion arises within you? Confidence? Discomfort? If it's the latter, it's a sign that you need to invest some time in it.

Think about how each skill informs your daily routine, decision-making process, and/or interaction with others. Where are you strongest? Where do you need to develop or improve? What action can you implement to strengthen your skills in your daily life as founder?

Exercise 31: Core Action Skills

Core Action Skills			
Skill	How often and how well do you employ this skill	Rate your skill (1 = weak; 2 = competent; 3 = strong; 4 = excellent)	Action to develop or refine
Initiate			
Plan			
Execute			

Core Action Skills			
Skill	How often and how well do you employ this skill	Rate your skill (1 = weak; 2 = competent; 3 = strong; 4 = excellent)	Action to develop or refine
Solve			
Lead			

Now you see where you're strongest in Core Action Skills and where you need to strengthen.

Next, take stock of where you stand with the following Core Management Skills.

The Founder's Core Management Skills
1. Self-management
2. Time management
3. Communication
4. Relationship management
5. Project management
6. Stress management
7. Crisis management
8. Financial management

All founders need these Core Management Skills. Now is a good time to review and assess. If you're already proficient, you've got a head start. If you feel tentative in certain areas, acknowledge them, then acquire confidence through practice. You don't need to excel at all of them before starting your venture (though it's great if you do), but you need to be proficient because they are essential to your success.

If there are areas where you feel you've already developed competency or expertise, skip them and move on to the next section.

Self-Management

As founder, you'll want to ensure you're able to manage personal and work fronts, before you can manage your crew and operation.

The Introspection exercises gave you a good sense of how your mind, body, heart, and spirit work together. They also illuminated the resources and habits you can tap for support, inspiration, and recharging, such as exercise, solitude, religious / spiritual practice, family, friends, and so on. They revealed areas you need to monitor or improve. In sum, they provided you with an integrated approach to self-management.

Time Management

As founder, you're creating not just a product, but also a company with complete with infrastructure, systems, and standards. You'll need good time management to make it happen in a timely way and keep it going.

Prior to founding your company, you might have been a professional in an established business. You might have found it easy to observe established working hours and deadlines. Now that you're at your own company, your work schedule will be yours. You're liberated from your structured corporate life. You may organize time as you see fit.

A first-time founder may experience a thrill of freedom, as work time is now under her control. After initial elation, she may find herself struggling to establish time management that works well. This is a common challenge for new founders.

As a new founder, you'll require more self-discipline than ever because you're the boss. You set and change schedules, deadlines, and performance metrics. Review how you spend your time, and plan to spend it wisely. You don't have time to waste; you want your business to run efficiently, and you must set an example. Research, assess, and customize your time management to your needs.

Founder Insights

View time as a friend instead of an adversary. Time is a resource, not something you have to conquer.

Recognize the difference between "urgent" and "important" and act accordingly. And note that a packed daily routine isn't necessarily an effective routine. You can be busy, but this doesn't mean that you're productive.

Respect your own time so you can set boundaries and make good use of it. If you don't set boundaries, others will and take away precious time from you.

Communication

As founder, you need to communicate well. A message not understood is a message not sent. Whether you're building a sole proprietorship or a Fortune 1000 company, communicating ideas effectively to your team, partners, and clients is key to success.

Founder Insights

We each communicate in our own unique way. It is important to know how you communicate as well as to recognize others' communication strengths and weaknesses.

Communication employs all your senses, and it's a two-way process. You can't communicate well if you don't listen well, if you're not attuned to your interlocutor's response. It is important to recognize how you deliver your message as well as how your audience responds to it. You need to be aware.

Relationship Management

You need others to aid you, whether you're creating an individual proprietorship or a Fortune 1000 company. Ask for help when you need and be prepared to help when you can, when you're asked to help. Building and maintaining relationships is essential.

Founder Insights

Think of your relationships as a garden. If you want them to grow, you need to tend to them. You only have so many hours in a day, so cultivate the ones that inspire, enhance, and/or give you a chance to contribute, to make a difference. Don't waste time on quantity. Jettison the negative ones that deplete you.

Project Management

Every project needs a plan—whether a 5-step or 20-step plan—to ensure successful completion. Each plan needs a competent manager to execute—someone thoughtful, responsive, organized, and resourceful; who sees both the forest and the trees; who delivers.

Excellent project management (PM) is a basic skill that should be taught in schools and required for anyone who embarks on a venture. Yet many founders don't take time to determine if they've good PM skills.

Many never establish PM standards. Some assume that individuals they hire for key positions—like head of sales, marketing, and client relations—are excellent project managers. Founders shouldn't assume this. You may have a great product idea, but without proficient project managers, you and your team will encounter serious glitches.

As founder, you will oversee activities that require competent project management. First, assess your own skill, and acknowledge where you need to improve. Establish standards and performance metrics. Allocate energy, time, and resources for project management from Day One. Without it, your venture will sail off course.

Founder Insights

Do not underestimate the importance of good project management. Your business needs all the parts working in concert. You need excellent project leaders to lead your team, establish meetings agendas, and manage the workflow that keeps your operation humming smoothly.

Stress Management

Starting a business is a thrilling and very stressful experience. Creating a new product, finding buyers, building a new team, and finding and allocating resources is not for the faint of heart. When you're a manager or a director, you're responsible for your department or section. When you're the founder, you're responsible for your entire crew and operation. Your stress level will increase. If you've already incorporated stress management habits into your daily life, that's great. If you've been struggling with this, now's the time to assess and prepare yourself.

Founder Insights

The harder you drive yourself and your team, the faster you'll achieve results. But if you don't take care of your own stress as founder and establish a stress management program for your team, you will burn out and so will they. Exhausted people do not make decisions clearly, nor do they perform to their potential.

Crisis Management

It's natural that an aspiring founder would be enthralled with his new business idea to the detriment of crisis management. But you will encounter crises, so you must think ahead, and develop or refine crisis management skills. Don't wait for a crisis to catch you unprepared.

Founder Insights

Envision and prepare for various worst-case scenarios:

- What would you do if you had to fire a co-founder who happens to be one of your best friends? Or if you had to fire a family member, and this person has invested heavily in your venture, or holds a key position?

- What would you do if a competitor claimed that you stole his business idea or technology, and you had to halt operation, pending arbitration and a huge adjustment in your business strategy?

- What would you do if your key supplier shut down suddenly? Or the promotional materials for an upcoming launch, which you had ordered from an online printer, had incorrect dates and pricing info? What if you had budgeted for a purchase insufficiently?

- What would you do if your top salesperson suddenly quit in the middle of negotiations with an important client?

Do you have the confidence and poise to respond to whatever crises may occur? Or are you simply hoping you won't run into XYZ problems because you won't know how to resolve them?

Knowing how to remain calm and maintain poise during crises is key. Don't make critical decisions during stressful moments. If you can, pause for a day, a week. Step away from the situation to obtain some perspective. Apply your personal powers: recognize you always have a choice. Even the least rewarding or the most difficult decision still entails a choice.

What skills, habits, and mental resources do you have at your disposal that will help you manage and solve crises?

Financial Management

In the Introspection section, you took stock of your personal financial habits. These will influence how you will deal with your company's finances. Now we take it one step further and help you prepare for your Finance role in your startup phase.

As founder, you are responsible for cash flow. You need to track expenses and revenues with an Excel spreadsheet or subscription to QuickBooks, an accounting software.

If your professional experience includes finance and accounting, you've got a head start. If you don't, that's all right, too. Most first-time entrepreneurs aren't CPAs either.

At a minimum, acquire basic proficiency so you know how to manage your company's money. When you can afford it, hire a bookkeeper and an accountant to help you manage finances and prepare for tax payments. As business grows, you may delegate this responsibility to your CFO.

Take an accounting course online or at your local community college to develop basic competency. Read books on financial management for new businesses. Keep in mind no one definitive resource works for all;

every expert should cover the basics but also offer their unique insights. The Internal Revenue Service is a deep resource for taxes.

Founder Insights

Always build in some financial cushion (especially if you're entering unfamiliar territory) for each project because most often, it will cost more than you originally anticipated. Double your estimates.

Assess Your Founder's Core Management Skills

Clarify your attitude. When you think of each of the following skills, what emotion arises within you? Confidence? Discomfort? If it's the latter, it's a sign that you need to invest some time in it.

Think about how each skill informs your daily routine, decision-making process, and/or interaction with others. Where are you strongest? Where do you need to develop or improve? What action can you implement to strengthen your skills in your daily life as founder?

Exercise 32: Core Management Skills

Core Management Skills			
Skill	How often and how well you employ this skill	Rate your skill (1 = weak; 2 = competent; 3 = strong; 4 = excellent)	Action to develop or refine
Self management			
Time management			

Core Management Skills			
Skill	How often and how well you employ this skill	Rate your skill (1 = weak; 2 = competent; 3 = strong; 4 = excellent)	Action to develop or refine
Communica-tion			
Relationship management			
Project management			
Stress management			
Crisis management			
Financial management			

In additional to Core Management Skills, you'll need the following Core Qualities to help you prepare well for all kinds of situations that may arise. Assess your strengths and determine where you need to improve.

The Founder's Core Qualities
1. Self-awareness
2. Self-reliance
3. Discernment
4. Adaptability
5. Steadfastness
6. Perseverance
7. Optimism
8. Empathy

Self-awareness

Developing self-awareness isn't the first task that comes to mind for aspiring founders, but it's essential. I've worked with founders who lacked this quality. They didn't know how they behaved and appeared as business owner; they didn't recognize their worth, strengths, and weaknesses. They made critical decisions driven by ego or knee-jerk reaction, which contributed to startup failure.

Much of this book focuses on helping you develop it. It's the best gift you can give yourself. Self-awareness is a lifelong pursuit that each should undertake. Being self-aware means knowing:

- Where you came from: who and what influenced you in your personal and professional growth.
- Why you do what you do: what motivates you, what shuts you down. Who you are, and who you are not, and who you want to become as you evolve.
- What conditions enable you to be your best and what factors bring out your worst.
- What you need to take care of yourself well so you can take care of others.
- What you want to achieve: how you go about accomplishing it, what you are willing (or not willing) to do to realize it.

The more self-aware you are, the more attuned you'll be to your values, purpose, goals, strengths, and weak spots as you conduct business.

The more self-aware you are, the more aware you are of yourself in relation to others—how you appear, communicate, solve, and collaborate with others, and how they respond to you.

The more self-aware you are, the more you'll see which skills and resources you still need to acquire for your venture.

Founder Insights

Self-awareness alone does not lead to action, for one also needs self-confidence and personal initiative to act and affect change. Yet lack of self-awareness will surely to lead to blunders, if not failure.

Self-reliance

A self-reliant individual is one who: 1) knows her own powers and how to manage them, 2) has faith in her own judgment, and 3) possesses confidence in her ability to accomplish goals. A self-reliant mindset means possessing inner resources, trusting yourself to be someone you can depend on completely. It means counting on yourself to make things happen, solve problems, and create forward momentum.

Picture yourself as a captain on the high seas. Your satellite tracking system stops working, and no one on board can fix it. Do you sit there adrift, or do you reach for your sextant? Training yourself to be self-reliant will prepare you to solve problems and keep your venture on course.

If you were a part of an established corporate entity, you had a support system that to helped you resolve a crisis. If one engineer got sick, another was available to substitute. If you needed research, your R&D department got it done. If you needed collateral, your marketing department produced them. If you needed a contract, your legal department cranked it out.

Most first-time founders will be bootstrapping during the first two years. You won't have a support system; you'll be the support system. You'll have to wear many hats while working with collaborators and suppliers.

Many inexperienced founders assume that help is a phone call or online search away. It's understandable, since today's technological offerings give us access to all kinds of immediate assistance. But many founders will experience crises when help isn't available because of lack of resources, money, or talent. While you may have advisors, friends, and family for advice, you'll experience many moments when you must take action alone.

Founder Insights

Self-reliance is not about not needing others' help; it's about ensuring you always have someone to rely on, especially during crises.

A self-reliant mindset sets the stage for your entrepreneurial journey so that you are emotionally, mentally, physically, and spiritually prepared to help yourself. It gives you a 24/7 Go-To person: you.

Discernment

A discerning individual possesses keen mental perception and understanding of people, situations, and environments. He can sift through hype and fluff to see what's beneath.

As founder, you'll need to navigate a sea of information overload, changing market conditions, and endless consumer demands. On a daily basis, you'll need to suss out the reality behind marketing and sales hype, recognize the difference between good and misplaced advice, and detect people's true motives behind false promises.

Adaptability

Founders need to be flexible and adapt to changes on their journey. Along with the willingness to adapt is the openness to change—and to ideas, solutions, and outcomes they might not have considered.

Some co-founders were so sold on their products they were unwilling to adapt to a new generation of consumers. One startup went from occupying the leader position in their market to falling behind because they refused to adapt to changing tastes.

Founders need to adapt or they may miss timely opportunities and take a tumble. Worse, if they're not open to change and fail to adapt, they may not survive.

Founder Insights

A part of being adaptable is knowing when it's prudent to adjust pace and path. It's knowing when you need to move and when you need to wait.

Like the sea captain who needs to adjust to changing weather, you may find that you'll need to adapt to sudden changes in suppliers, market conditions, customer tastes, and technology.

Steadfastness

As founder, you may face changing customer tastes that force you to reassess your course. You may encounter crises that threaten to bring down your business. You'll need faith, a steady mind, and stout heart to stay firm in your purpose and conviction, and to focus on problem solving.

As you build your business, you'll need help from family, friends, former colleagues, collaborators, and suppliers. As you depend on them to be responsive and reliable to help you succeed, you'll need to return the favor and demonstrate the same kind of dependability.

Founder Insights

Be unwavering in your purpose, steadfast in your pursuit of your vision. Avoid external distractions.

Demonstrate your firm commitment and unwavering support to anyone from whom you expect such reciprocity.

Perseverance

The entrepreneurial voyage is always longer than what most first-time founders anticipate. It requires perseverance.

You'll experience operational glitches, supply delays, hardware malfunctions, employee grievances, and hacking.

Potential business partners and investors may reject you. You may come across non-believers who question everything about you, your product, and your venture.

You must hold your course, persevere through rough patches, solve your problems, and move forward.

Founder Insights

In the startup landscape, problems need to be resolved quickly. Speed is expected and so is perseverance. Yet speed takes center stage while perseverance plods along silently behind, until results are delivered. In the end, what matters the most is faith in your entrepreneurial journey and willingness to endure—including through challenging times. These are what it takes to realize your dream.

Optimism

An optimist views a situation, condition, or event favorably. She leans toward the view that all will end on a positive note.

It is easy to be enthusiastic and positive when you're starting out. When you encounter obstacles and lose momentum, that's when you need faith. You'll need an optimist's resolve to find a silver lining and solutions. You'll need an optimist's confidence to create momentum and kick-start a stalled process. Pessimists have a harder time moving past challenges.

Martin Seligman, a psychologist at the University of Pennsylvania, has researched happiness and found that optimism and pessimism are learned behaviors. If you're a pessimist, think about how your responses to past challenges turned out. Were results satisfactory?

If you note a pattern of unsatisfactory results based on your outlook, step away from your comfort zone and think how an optimist would respond or act. But don't be a Pollyanna; wearing rose-colored glasses doesn't work either.

Founder Insights

As founder, you must cultivate optimism and be your own cheerleader. Your venture is your dream, your vision. If you don't have an optimist's outlook, you won't be able to rally and convince others in your company to stay and support you during difficult times.

Last, but not least...

Empathy

As founder, you'll interact with all kinds of individuals; they include those you hire to be your crew, your strategic partners, suppliers, consultants, and investors. Your ability to identify with other people's thoughts, feelings, and view points—putting yourself in their shoes— will help you to communicate and manage various relationships better.

Evaluate Your Founder's Core Qualities

Clarify your attitude. When you think of each of the following qualities, what emotion arises within you? Confidence? Discomfort? If it's the latter, it's a sign that you need to invest some time in it.

Think about how each quality informs your daily routine, decision-making process, and/or interaction with others. Where are you strongest? Where do you need to develop or improve? What action can you implement to strengthen your skills in your daily life as founder?

Exercise 33: Core Qualities

Core Qualities			
Quality	How often and how well do you tap into this quality	Rate your level (1 = weak; 2 = competent; 3 = strong; 4 = excellent)	Action to develop or refine
Self-awareness			
Self-reliance			
Discernment			
Adaptability			
Steadfastness			
Perseverance			

Core Qualities			
Quality	How often and how well do you tap into this quality	Rate your level (1 = weak; 2 = competent; 3 = strong; 4 = excellent)	Action to develop or refine
Optimism			
Empathy			

If you need to strengthen one or two critical founder skills, you can manage this while starting your company. If, after reflection, research, and assessment, you conclude you still have five or more skills to develop, you should consider taking classes, self-teaching, or a job where you can acquire these while getting paid. You may be courageous for wanting to "wing it" by starting your venture without many critical skills, but you should avoid taking the helm without having developed competency in most of them. It's wise to spend time training and being prepared.

Startup Anecdotes

I worked for five established companies— an investment bank, a management consulting firm, two wireless service providers, and a family business—before starting my first venture. I learned about infrastructure, standards of operations, processes, and different corporate cultures and management styles. I picked up best practices and pitfalls to avoid. These helped me set up my first operation without startup chaos.

That said, starting a new business is one thing, but running it is another. I discovered that even though I was in charge, I lacked certain functional skills.

I had built a new company and knew I had to promote it, but I tensed each time I thought of business development. I understood why I chafed at selling; I had grown up in a culture that prizes academic achievement and relegates selling to the bottom of the ladder. The stereotype about sleazy sales people was ingrained in my psyche.

I spent time reading, talking to mentors, and trying to improve my sales skills. I struggled to wear the Sales hat without feeling I was faking it. I learned to leverage my natural instinct to be helpful, and I looked for opportunities where I could contribute. It took me a long time to stop cringing at contacting potential clients. Today I would say I've developed competency, but I'd never hire myself as head of a business development team. It's not my forte, but neither is it my Achilles heel.

So, if you know what your weak spot is, commit time and energy to addressing it.

The Founder's Financial Preparedness

You've examined your financial habits. Now review your financial situation, and think about how your venture will affect your financial standing.

Exercise 34: Financial Preparedness

1. How much money have you saved?
2. How much money will you set aside and not touch, under ANY circumstances?
3. How much money do you need to cover monthly basic needs while you work on your venture?
4. How much money will you invest to start your venture?
5. Will you invest to keep it going until break-even or profitable stage?

6. At what point will you stop financing your business if your product doesn't attract buyers?
7. How much money will you allocate for emergency needs for the venture?
8. At what point will you need to raise money? How much do you plan to raise? How much of your company would you give up?
9. How will you use the proceeds?
10. Ultimately, how much control of the company do you plan to maintain?
11. When do you expect to see a return on your investment? In five years? Ten years?

If you plan to finance your business, you're in complete financial control of your operation.

If you plan to seek additional money you'll need to explore different financial options: bank loan, SBA loan, friends and family loan, crowd sourcing, angel investment, and venture capital. You'll need to research and understand how each option works, how your venture may benefit, and how much ownership you will have to give up.

Familiarize yourself with the financial landscape before you start your venture. Be informed before you offer equity to a co-founder or a new team member. Understand what you're giving away, when you raise money.

Plan ahead. Let's say that in Year 3 or Year 4, you decide that the entrepreneurial life is not for you. Will you have set aside money—money not allocated for the venture? Will you have a financial cushion while you're taking a break while or looking for another job?

You'll find many books on financial management for startups. Spend time studying them if you need additional education. Research online. Visit your library. Don't start your venture without this competency.

The Founder's Industry Experience

Every job you've ever performed has contributed to where you are today. There's value in learning what you're good at and discovering what doesn't suit you. Take out your most recent resume. Review it, and update it. Extract for the following exercise.

- What experience and insights did you obtain from the industries that you've worked in?
- Which industry knowledge and experience can you apply to your founder role?
- What new experience and skills will you need to develop for your venture?

Exercise 35: Industry Experience

Industry Experience		
Industry	Functional experience / skill	Achievement / Failure / Insight
1.		
2.		
3.		

You will have more resources and insights at your disposal, if you possess deep knowledge of the industry in which you're planning to sell your product.

It may be worthwhile to acquire industry experience by working for someone else first. Otherwise, you'll have to spend time, energy, money, and resources learning an entirely new market niche.

The Founder's Survival Skills

You're probably excited about your new business idea and raring to start developing it. Survival skills aren't on your to-do list. But proper planning prevents poor performance. Know what survival tools do you need in addition to founder competency skills and qualities.

Many inexperienced founders rarely give much thought to what may go wrong. Many have this simplistic view of the road to success: build the prototype, find paying customers, build a client base, find investors, and expand. But unexpected problems loom large, and small problems crop up all along the way.

You can't prepare for all scenarios, but as founder, your self-reliant mindset and survival skills will help you face challenges.

You need to envision the best outcome, the realistic outcome, and the worst outcome. Conduct scenario planning. What can go wrong while you're on the high seas? What do you need to do if you lack tools to fix a leak or run out of supplies, or have to deal with a troublesome crew member? How will you resolve worst-case scenarios?

You've spent time in the Introspection section reacquainting yourself with your sources of influence, beliefs, values, habits, and purpose. You've identified powers and strengths. You've recalled successes and failures.

You need resources that you can access any time, anywhere: those resources reside within you. As you progress through this book and accompanying exercises, think about what to add to your Survival Kit.

Example: Founder Brooke's Survival Kit
• Excellence with logistics • Tactile skills • Negotiation skills • Patience • Optimism • Self-reliance • Calm and poise during crisis • Unconventional ways of doing things

Exercise 36: Founder's Survival Kit

Over the next few weeks, think about what you will add to your Survival Kit. What are your must-haves?

CHAPTER RECAP

As founder, you need competency to start, run your operation, and troubleshoot in emergencies. In this chapter, you've focused on developing founder competency, which included thinking through the four phases of your venture, assessing your core skills and qualities, allocating time to train yourself, preparing financially, and gathering skills and tools for your Survival Kit.

You've also had an opportunity to think about how you'll fortify your founder's worth. First-time founders seldom realize that their worth is something that they need to articulate, affirm, and build throughout their entrepreneurial journey. For many, because they are unaware of it, they inadvertently give potential investors an edge. Define your worth before someone else does it for you.

Give yourself time to prepare. You want to assume the helm competently and confidently.

Chapter V:
Establish a Foundation for Your Startup

The second part of your manifest focuses on your startup. As founder, you need to develop and run your Operation. But as product originator, you need to focus on developing your Product. You need to research and prepare for these two roles in tandem, before starting your venture. You need to attend to both operation and product from the start because they intertwine.

First-time founders often focus exclusively on their product idea, believing it will carry their company to success. Many overlook their founder role and the need to captain the entire ship and not just oversee their product. They're either unaware or choose to delay the need to create a structure to support their product and operation through the whole of their entrepreneurial journey. By the time they decide to focus on this task, they have to backtrack to incorporate all kinds of data and development tasks into their product and overall business strategies. This section will help you avoid this mistake.

Every founder possesses unique values, skills, talents, and experiences. Study the following Operation and Product sections. Extract what is appropriate for your venture. Create a list of issues you need to research for in-depth knowledge. Decide which skills you need to strengthen or develop.

The Operation Section

This section gives you a framework; once you've read it, you will know how to build your business. Each new founder must research, think about, and develop the following three operation-related areas, in order to be assume the helm well prepared:

- Global Issues
- People
- Infrastructure

Address Global Issues

With an integrated mindset, you need to address two global issues that affect all aspects of your product and business before embarking on your journey: your company's brand identity and your company's cultural norms. The reason they are "global" is whenever you make changes to them, a ripple effect occurs throughout your operation.

Develop Your Brand Identity

A company's brand is its reputation. For example, Patek Philippe watches attract individuals who favor best of the best, continuity, tradition, and timeless elegance. Timex Ironman watches represent athleticism, endurance, and functionality. A $25 Cassio is about price.

Your brand is intertwined with your company's identity—its name, business and product description, core values, purpose, personality traits, and emotional appeal.

The name, business description, and brand identity you choose for your business will dictate how you create and present your product, whether high-end or low-end. They'll dictate how you create and position your brand, market it, prepare promotional materials, and develop sales pitches. Adjustments to these "global" components will affect your entire business.

Say you want to create a high-end product that sells only at Barney's; the language that your brand strategist uses will target a high-end customer segment. The materials in your product and its packaging will reflect a high-end sensibility. If you change your mind and decide to sell at a lower price at Target, you'll need to change your branding and marketing messages to reach Target customers. This change will affect your product materials, your packaging materials, your marketing collateral, your sales pitches, and more.

As founder, you're responsible for creating brand identity that permeates all aspects of your operation. Your identity comprises the following factors, so reflect and research carefully.

Company Name

Your new company's name will reflect your venture's mission and purpose. It will reflect your values, aesthetics, and aspirations. It needs to resonate with your target audience. It needs to suit the market that you're trying to enter, whether highbrow, lowbrow, or middlebrow.

In practical terms, your new company's name is going to be subject to what's available with your state's business registration office and with a domain name registry. You don't want to choose a name that is unavailable.

Startup Anecdotes

I once worked with a startup that spent millions of dollars on product development—a social networking platform. When the executive team was ready to release its alpha site to a few thousand chosen users, they discovered that someone else had registered for their desired domain name. By then they were convinced that their chosen domain was a must-have and paid over $200K for it. Sadly, the startup tanked within that first year of alpha testing. They never even went into beta.

Choosing the right name requires testing and revision. You want to settle on one that affirms your purpose and inspires you and your audience. You want one that's easy to spell, pronounce, and remember.

For example, Living Homes is an appropriate name for a Southern California company that builds eco-friendly houses designed to optimize construction materials soil, water, and energy consumption.

Business Description
Describe your company and product in one or two concise sentences. Or answer this question, "What service or product does your business offer, and who are your customers?"

- One-line company description _____
- One-line product description _____

Purpose
Why does your company exist? Your purpose can be measurable or intangible. It may be to eradicate a disease or to empower people through education. It may be to provide a product or a service for the elderly. While your product line, your marketing strategy, or your sales strategy can change over time, your purpose should remain unchanged. Your purpose should serve as an aspiration as well as inspiration; as such, it will shape your culture, strategy, and goals. It will serve as your beacon when you feel lost at sea.

Should your business' purpose align with or mirror your personal purpose? I believe it should, based on my years in the startup trenches. For during tough times, if you don't feel aligned with your organization's purpose, you'll have difficulty motivating yourself and wonder why it's hard to move things along.

I've worked with co-founders who were motivated by the lure of extreme wealth, but were emotionally unconnected to their creation. When things got tough, they didn't have commitment or passion to persevere.

Your venture's purpose needs to be succinct. One sentence will do it. Examples of purpose:

- To help X group of individuals improve their livelihood through education.
- To entertain and bring laughter to people.
- To helps save lives (with your new tool or service).

Core Values

Your venture's core values should reflect your personal values. If you ascribe core values to your venture without believing in them, your actions won't reflect your beliefs. You're starting with a handicap.

Your core values should connect closely to your purpose. Unlike mission statements, core values, like purpose, are immutable.

It's important to reflect and define what these values mean to you, if you are to convey them clearly to team members, customers, suppliers, and strategic partners. When they aren't articulated clearly, you'll encounter miscommunication and operational issues.

What do you value? Examples:

- You value people > People come first.
- You value education > Education for all.
- You value humor > Humor/laughter brings people together.
- You value nature > Clean water, clean air, clean grounds.

Personality Traits

Each business entity has its own personality. The personality traits you assign to your business will appeal to your target audience. Think of archetypal roles, such as healer for healthcare products or teacher for educational tools or programs.

Vision

Your vision is where you want your venture to go, while your purpose is why your venture exists. Your vision should be expansive and include the following:

1. What's your vision for your business? Your vision should reflect your zeal and your ambitions. Examples:
   - Become the leading builder of LEED-certified dwellings.
   - Become the leading advocate for excellent elder care.

2. What is your vision for your brand identity?
   - What personality traits will you assign to it?
   - Does it represent an ideal, a value, and/or an archetype?

3. How extensive do you envision your reach to be?
   - Do you want to sell your products to a narrow segment?
   - Do you want to reach every household in the U.S. or all over the world?

4. What is your vision of your business' location and size?
   - Do you plan to build a local business, a regional entity, or a global enterprise?
   - Will it be brick and mortar, multi-channel retailer, or an e-commerce?

5. What is your vision for your business structure?
   - Do you plan to operate it as a proprietorship, a partnership, or a public company?

6. What is your vision of the individuals who will work with you, for you?
   - What kind of personalities and backgrounds do they possess?
   - What kind of values do they have?
   - What kind of functional and intangible skills do you require of them?

7. How long is your envisioned journey? Is it a five-year run? Or is it a business that you want to operate until you retire?

Your purpose, core values, and vision influence all components of your business: brand identity, goals, strategies, tactics, structures, standards, and processes. Clear articulation with continual and strategic reinforcement will keep you on course. Give yourself time to reflect, research, and revise until your answers feel right to you.

Exercise 37: Create Brand Identity

Venture's Identity - Checklist	
Company name and domain name	
Business description • One-line company description • One-line product description	
Purpose	
Core values	
Personality traits	
Vision • Vision for venture • Vision for brand identity • Vision of market reach • Vision of location and size • Vision for business structure • Vision of team members • Vision for exit	

Your brand is your reputation, which is influenced by your identity, your presentation, your performance, your visibility, and your community. Establish a brand management program that incorporates these factors.

Exercise 38: Manage Your Brand

Think about all the components that reflect and affect your brand.

Your presentation and appearance include:
- How you present your venture's identity through your company name, business description, purpose, vision, and core values.
- How you and your employees present yourselves, products, marketing collateral, and sales pitches. As founder, you're the first and leading representative of your company's brand. What are you representing and how you are representing it to the world?

Your performance includes:
- How well your product delivers its promise.
- How your product's performance stacks up against competition.
- How well you manage relationships: how you and your employees interact with one another, with vendors, partners, customers, even competitors. How well the structure and systems you have in place for your entire organization support you and your team. How well your team performs in various functional roles: product development, engineering, marketing, finance, business development, and operations.
- How well your chosen technology performs for your customers, your team, and you.
- How well your team handles your corporate social responsibility.

Your visibility includes:
- What you are showcasing to the world: your product, your people, and your company.
- Where you appear online and in the real world.
- How often your company and product receive media coverage and what type of media coverage.

Your community includes:
- your internal team
- your customers
- your suppliers
- your strategic partners and investors
- your critics and your competitors.

Create a plan to monitor your brand's performance monthly, quarterly, and annually. Focus on your company, people, and product. Are you conveying a consistent message? Monitor your performance, review feedback, and institute appropriate changes.

Startup Anecdotes

Richard was a corporate lawyer who decided to set up his own business. He was my client from another project and we had worked well together. He engaged me to take charge of his brand identity. Over a summer, we worked with a designer to define his company's visual identity and articulate its purpose. We discussed how he wanted to present himself and his work, and which customer segments he wanted to target. Richard was an outdoor enthusiast, so we incorporated elements of nature and the San Francisco Presidio—his office's location—into his brand identity.

The result included a complete visual identity suite: a well designed logo with an image that pays tribute to natural settings inside The Presidio, a concise tag line, business cards, stationery, marketing materials, and a website that reflected the brand and showcased Richard's client portfolio and endorsements. Most important was how the end result aligned deeply with what Richard wanted to convey: his values and accomplishments, services he was offering, projects he wanted to pursue, and the types of clients he wanted to attract.

Address Your Brand Early

Your brand development should begin as soon as you start thinking about your business idea. As that idea takes shape, so does your brand.

Develop your brand in tandem with your product; your brand's DNA should be present in all components of your venture. At a minimum, you need to ensure you're starting out aligned. Founders, company, and product need to represent the brand consistently. It sounds like common sense, but many founders ignore this or are unaware of its importance.

Your brand and content strategy go together. Content you create for your venture—company name, purpose, values, logo, product (design, features, functionality, and performance), marketing messages, sales tools, customer service training guides, websites, and smart phone apps—should reflect your brand's identity. You may include other elements, such as texture, sound, smell, color, lighting, and location.

If you offer your product to diverse demographics, you'll need to think about how your brand will appear to consumers from other cultures and in other languages. You don't want your logo to spell "useless" in Swahili.

Brand development can take months, depending on vision, size, and budget resources. Don't wait until you're six months into your venture or in the middle of product development before you give attention to your brand. This is the most common branding error committed by inexperienced founders.

Brand development is a continual process where insights from product feedback, customer service input, consumer research, market research, competitive knowledge, and industry trends are fed back into your management information system. From time to time, these are adjusted.

Think about how you'll create your brand identity. Take charge of it, develop it, and monitor its reputation. Ensure that you're conveying a consistent message across the board.

Establish Your Culture

Your business will have its own culture, whether you intend to run it for a few years or until you retire.

The primary influential factor is you—your personality will set the tone. Thus far, we have focused this book on you—the founder. Your new self-awareness should help you understand how you will influence new team members.

We read about successful entrepreneurs advising, "Hire the best people, and get out of their way." Indeed, you should hire the most qualified that you can afford. But before you begin delegating, you need standards, systems, and processes in place. These provide structure and order for newcomers.

As founder, you provide guidance and instruction to those you hire, so they can embrace the culture you've established. If you don't, your culture will develop by default and may not turn out to reflect what you had in mind. You may envision a culture of execution, but if you don't articulate your expectations, confusion, and chaos may reign.

The Introspection exercises provided you with clarity regarding your standards, work habits, and preferred environment. Here's your opportunity to design your culture and attract the personalities that suit it.

Even if your business comprises both local and remote team members, it's essential that you communicate to all who come aboard your cultural norms—the definitions, standards, processes, and performance metrics that they all need to observe.

- Definitions
- Standards and Processes
- Metrics

Many first-time founders do not invest time and energy into articulating what kind of culture they want to develop. This is a great time to think hard and obtain clarity regarding your requirements.

Definitions

Create your culture by defining the type of environment you want to establish and by articulating your values, purpose, and vision to your team members. This includes providing clear definitions of concepts related to starting and operating a business.

Definitions are important because when you share them with your team, everyone is on the same page and this prevents misunderstandings.

These following words appear often in startup conversations, yet you'd be surprised how often people on the same team have different definitions of the same words. Ask yourself, "What do these words and concepts mean to me as founder?" and provide your answers.

- What does "service" mean?
- What does "product" mean?
- What does "obtaining traction" mean?
- What does "break-even" mean?
- What does "profitability" mean?
- What constitutes "excellence?"

Startup Anecdotes

I worked as a brand strategist for a startup that created an online tool for its customers. I asked each founding team member to complete the same branding exercise, which included questions about their company's purpose, product, competitive advantages, pricing strategies, customer segments, and support.

When I shared the results, team members were surprised to learn that their answers were far from identical. Until then, they had assumed they were on the same page.

One example. Team members were asked to envision and describe their customer support process. Does service begin when the customer lands on the Home page? Does it begin after the customer has purchased the tool and downloaded it? What type of support will they provide? A Frequently Asked Questions page? Instant chat service? Email? A toll-free number? A follow-up email to confirm purchase and download, with links to support and customer feedback?

The exercises helped them realize how their different views were affecting their venture's brand positioning, which in turn affected the company's product development, marketing, sales, and customer support. With new insights, the founders also revised their budget.

When starting out, don't assume you're all speaking the same language. Articulate and clarify to ensure you're on the same page.

You'll want clear definitions so that: 1) you can establish standards and metrics, and 2) you can communicate in a uniform, consistent way to your team members, investors, vendors, strategic partners, and customers. Consequently, they'll know what to expect from your team and you.

Standards and Processes

Define standards and establish processes; they reflect what you value and will support the culture that you want to build. Keep in mind that you may hire the most qualified professionals to help you build your business, but if you don't have a vision, standards, processes, and metrics in place, you'll find yourself with miscommunication, mismanagement, and chaos. You won't have a unified crew to help you move forward seamlessly.

Startup Anecdotes

Two co-founders wanted to create a community-building site. They hired five different engineering firms to build the platform and embed features like group membership, a messaging service, a photo-sharing time line, and voicemail translation to email. (This was before online platform providers like Ning and long before Facebook's time line and messaging services.) I was product manager for the group membership component, which one of these firms was to provide.

The co-founder/CEO Jake got all the consultants on a conference call and told us what he wanted from each firm. Jake had hired a designer to create wire frames and those were the blueprints shared with the team. For six months, in spite of constant requests for instructions, Jake couldn't settle on a style guide, so each firm ended up applying its own style.

Jake didn't share a project plan with assigned tasks and deadlines, showing how he envisioned what components would be. He didn't use any project management tool like Basecamp or basic Excel. In addition, no one on his executive team created a centralized place to store project assets.

Jake wanted to be involved in the development of every feature. He tracked progress by holding twice weekly Go-To-Meeting conference calls with the five teams, scheduled by his assistant. When project leaders asked for an agenda, she would reply, "It's whatever Jake wants to address." Fourteen people working on five different features attended the conference calls, during which Jake would do most of the talking. Half the people would sign off without having issues addressed.

Consequently, Jake was overloaded with requests for clarification, feedback, and approval. He left each project leader waiting days for answers. The teams collaborated as well as they could, but with many issues waiting for Jake's approval, the venture chugged along with delays.

Finally, when all the teams gathered to integrate their respective features into the main platform, there were only two companies that integrated successfully. The remaining three features didn't function properly.

We launched a barely functioning alpha site. New users tested the site and found glitches everywhere; they could not use the voice mail feature and had trouble creating the photo time line and music uploads. Complaints started rolling in, and senior management scrambled to set up an emergency customer support team. Jake had promised the clients a first-class ride with "killer apps," but he delivered a third-rate experience.

I've never worked in a startup that failed on so many levels, including leadership, team management, communications, time management, project management, and customer service.

Lessons for the founder: it's your responsibility to lead and manage your crew. You need to create and communicate your vision, project plan, processes and standards, and your performance metrics to each member who steps on board.

You'll remember that in the Introspection chapter, you reviewed and assessed your habits and many of the following management skills, and thought about how, as founder, you might apply them. Review these issues below and articulate what you'll do for your new operation, and how components will integrate.

Work Habits and Style
What kind of standards will you establish for yourself and your team in your venture?
- What does a work day (hours, team meetings, dress code, and protocols) at your company look like?
- What kind of performance do you expect from yourself and your team members?

Work Rhythm and Productivity
You already know your own rhythm and productivity pattern.
- How will you deal with other people's different productivity patterns?
- What performance standards will you implement in your venture for yourself and your team? What expectations will you convey?

Work Environment
You've reviewed your own preferred work environment.
- What kind of cultural environment will you establish? Formal or informal? People-oriented? Process-oriented? Data-oriented? Other / some combination?
- What kind physical environment will you create?
- Will you allow team members to telecommute and if you do, what requirements will you establish?

Time Management
In the Introspection section, you reviewed how you spend your time. You've identified patterns and taken note of how you prioritize. What kind of time management standards and processes will you implement for your team?

Communication Process
You've already assessed your communication skills. As you review the following, think about the standards and processes you want to establish for your new company.
- Some founders communicate best in person. Others stay connected by phone, by email, etc. What's your preferred method?
- Should all team members be required to write well?
- Should everyone be trained in presentation skills and in cross-cultural communications?
- What are your standards and processes for communicating progress updates and change / supply requests internally?
- What's your process for communicating with clients?

Relationship Management
In your Introspection exercises, you reviewed both your internal and external relationship management skills. What insights can you extract and apply to your business? What standards and processes will you establish for:
- your internal team
- your customers
- your suppliers
- your strategic partners
- your investors.

Project Management
As in the previous chapter, good PM skills are required of everyone on your team. Having done the exercise, you know where you're strong and where you need to improvement in to PM skills. You'll need to establish standards and performance metrics for those you plan to hire.

Financial Management

From your Introspection exercises, you updated your perspective on budgeting skills and spending habits. What kind of financial standards and management process will you establish for yourself as founder and your team members?

Stress Management

You've had an opportunity to assess how you manage your own stress in the Introspection exercises. What kind of stress management support will you establish for yourself and your team?

Crisis Management

In the previous chapter, you reviewed your crisis management skills.

- What insights did you cull and what can you incorporate into your founder role?
- What crisis management tools will you have in place for your team?

Give yourself some time to reflect and create standards and processes for your new business.

Metrics

Successful businesses are successful for many reasons, including because they have performance metrics.

Many startups don't establish performance metrics. Some who do aren't thorough, especially those who build to flip. Many have vague goals regarding their product. When the product development process encounters glitches, metrics are forgotten.

I've not encountered one startup where a product or company launched on the original target date. They were a week to more than a year late. This doesn't mean that founders should ignore goals, milestones, and metrics. But they should be aware of the runaway nature of a startup operation and monitor progress closely.

Startup Anecdotes

One CEO began his calendar year with monthly, quarterly, and annual goals. He would conduct team meetings twice a week. At the beginning of the week, a short meeting (in person and via Skype) to get the team on board regarding the week's team and individual goals. At the end of the week, he had a longer meeting to update and reset for the following week. Team members shared ideas that were working and processes that needed to be refined. They shared their work progress as well as insights about various clients. As the venture grew, team members from each department reported to their managers or directors.

A monthly wrap-up and a quarterly team meeting were in place to track company performance and individual achievements. The founder liked to recognize individual team members for accomplishments. As this founder also believed in transparency, at the end of each month, the entire team knew how many new clients were acquired, how much was generated in revenues, whether they were meeting monthly goals, and what they could expect at the end of the year in terms of compensation if the entire team continued to perform well. This regimen worked.

You'll need to establish a culture of execution, which includes metrics for the following areas:
- Individual and team performances
- Organizational performance
- Product performance
- Financial performance.

It is important to create a culture and structure that will support your operation before you start bringing new team members on board. This includes clarifying definitions and establishing standards, processes, and metrics. You may revise them as you progress, but it's important that you communicate the same guidelines and expectations to each new team member. You'll avoid miscommunication and operational glitches that beset disorganized startups.

Exercise 39: Establish Your Cultural Norms

Culture Checklist
Focus on: definitions, standards, processes, and metrics. • Define key words and concepts to establish common ground for new hires. • Articulate what kind of culture and work environment you wish to establish. • Establish work standards, processes, and metrics for: communication, project management, team management, financial management, stress management, and crisis management.

You are creating an environment that will support and nurture all the individuals you bring on board. Think about how your culture promotes sharing, collaboration, recognition, and rewards.

As founder, you need to be aware of these global issues and address them before embarking on your venture—in particular, before you start focusing most of your energy on your business idea, concept refinement, and product development. If you jump straight to product without spending substantial time on your global issues, you'll create a headache for yourself later. The need to include new information into your product and business halfway through development will be painful.

Choose Your Technology
Many new founders assume that they need the latest technology. This makes sense if they plan to build a product or service that caters to early adopters. In reality, you'll find many industry niches with customers who lag behind technologically.

Startup Anecdotes

I worked on a project where the startup team was building online tools such as video podcasts and personalized photo streaming for a specific client with thousands of users. While all the developers employed the latest computer operating systems and software, no one thought about the end-user's experience.

When the startup launched the service, many excited users experienced glitches because they were using older laptops, with older operating systems and browser versions. Podcasts wouldn't play, and photos wouldn't load. A quick survey revealed that less than 20 percent of the alpha users owned the latest computers and operating systems. The developers had to scale back their deliverables to accommodate both new and older versions.

Exercise 40: Choose Your Technology

Research and decide which technological tools work best for your new company.
1. What technology do you need to operate your business during start phase, and subsequent years? How do you intend to keep up with innovations? Will planned obsolescence be a part of your strategy?
2. What technological tools do your targeted customers use? What are their usage habits?

3. Research what hardware, software, and online services are right for your business model—whether it is a catering business, an elderly care business, or an online service business. What do you need and what can you afford?

Determine the costs and incorporate them into your budget.

Founder Insights

We live in a technology-driven world where founders are expected to use the latest software and hardware. Bootstrapping should be the starting mindset; it's prudent to use what you have at your disposal from the start and slowly add what you need. Avoid rushing to invest in the latest technology unless your business model requires it. Discover what technological tools your clients use or don't use, and plan appropriately.

Define Your Corporate Social Responsibility (CSR)
Part of being an integrated founder and creating an integrated operation with an integrated mindset is thinking about your organization's effect on the world.

More than ever, what we produce needs to be eco-friendly. If your product is physical and requires packaging, think about the materials used and how your customers will dispose them—whether in a recycling bin or one destined for landfill. Eco-friendliness extends beyond the physical product. Is what you're creating going to enhance your customer's environment and experience? Or will it diminish it?

Corporate Social Responsibility (CSR) refers to a company's business standards and ethics, and its impact on the environment and on positive social change.

Exercise 41: Define Corporate Social Responsibility

1. Define what corporate social responsibility means to your venture.
2. What kind of program will you create, how will you implement, and monitor its performance?

You may not have the resources to create a program when you're starting out as a team of one or of three. Keep CSR in mind for the right opportunity to execute and make it an integral part of your venture's operation. Giving back is something that enhances spirit company-wide.

•••

In sum, Global Issues apply to your product as well as your operation. Remember the ripple effect when you make changes to them.

Find the Right People

The second major area that you want to focus on is the people. This section shall focus on internal and external teams. You may have a great business idea, but if you don't have the right people to help you implement it, your business won't succeed.

Geoff Smart and Randy Street, authors of *Who - Solving Your #1 Problem*, cited talent management as the most significant factor when asked, "What makes a successful business?"[15]

If you've not been a hiring manager, acquire basic competence when creating a job posting, interviewing, and hiring.

Research the following issues and establish your Talent Management Blueprint before you hire your second employee. You'll avoid backtracking, if you invest time and energy in a well thought-out program.

Understand Labor Laws and Hiring Practices
Familiarize yourself with current employment laws, if you don't have a background in human resources and labor law. Be informed about hiring practices to avoid pitfalls.

Visit this resource and educate yourself: The U.S. Equal Employment Opportunity Commission. Your state government should have a website with information on starting a business and required state filings.

Acquire Knowledge of Equity Compensation Structure
In Chapter I, I recommended that you study financing options to understand ways to raise money and to compensate startup employees. Review your findings and establish your compensation structure.

Hire the Right People
Why do you need the right people? As founder, you'll need to run a tight ship during your first few years. Every individual you bring on board will play a critical role in your operation. You cannot afford to have a team with incompatible values and goals, or mismatched habits and skills.

Startup Anecdotes

I've worked with founders who were overwhelmed by their to-dos. Consequently, they didn't allocate time to assess needs and create their hiring criteria.

They rushed through the hiring process, placing too much emphasis on business and technical skills. They didn't make time to verify alignment on values, goals, habits, standards, and attitudes toward work and life. They didn't share company cultural norms, standards, and expectations with candidates.

Some founders delegate the entire hiring process to outsourced recruiters who don't possess understanding of the founders' values, attitudes, habits, standards, processes and/or style. The recruiter applies
his own lens and, of course, candidates suit the recruiter more than
the founder. This isn't the recruiters' fault; it's the founders' fault for
not taking time to communicate succinctly. In my early startup years,
I've been interviewed for projects where I wasn't a good fit because
the recruiter didn't get what the founder wanted; this was apparent
during the interviews.

Beware of this common misstep by new founders: hiring people
who possess the right skills, but the wrong values, attitudes or work
ethic. Results: worker frustration, project delays, wasted resources,
and high turnover.

Reflect before you answer the following questions.

Exercise 42: Define What the "Right" People Means to You

1. What kind of individuals do you want to have in your life, day
   after day? Think about the individuals who have been excellent
   collaborators and teachers.
2. What kind of individuals do you want and need to support you?
3. Do you require that they understand and share your values,
   your vision, and your purpose?
4. Do you care if their attitudes and habits align or don't align with
   yours?
5. Do you care if their work habits and processes differ from yours?
6. Do you want people to complement your personality? Or would
   you prefer to have people who are more like you?
7. Do the individuals need a certain educational and/or industry
   background?

8. What are your absolute must-haves and your deal-breakers for hiring and retaining?
9. How well do you think this candidate will represent your brand?

There are no right or wrong answers. But the more you know yourself and what you need in a team, the higher the chance you'll find the right people for you.

Once you find the right people, avoid taking them for granted, and avoid abusing their goodwill. Goodwill is like trust. Once it's compromised, it's hard to recover. Loss of goodwill—including trust and respect—can lead to venture failure.

Startup Anecdotes

The right time and place brought together one set of startup team members. Founder-CEO Jerry met one of his future developers and client relations manager at an alumni networking event. Many meetings ensued, during which Jerry touted the importance of having the right and best people on his team as well as his policy of always taking care of his people first. Weeks later, he hired Adam to work on the app side of the business and client relations manager Cameron to take charge of new clients.

In the first few months, the new team members gradually synchronized with the original startup team members; a working rhythm was established.

Soon Cameron started noticing that even though Jerry often sought team members' opinions about the company's brand identity, marketing pitch, and price points during weekly meetings, he always stuck to his own position.

Team members observed how Jerry would say, "I defer to your expertise" and then override various managers' decisions. Jerry ignored good advice on how to refine the product, pricing structures, sales tools, and client relations. Team members started voicing their frustration among themselves; everyone felt it was Jerry's way or the highway.

Tension between Jerry and team members increased, when Jerry started paying people late. At first, he was a month behind, then two, then three. When prompted, Jerry kept mentioning new accounts that were "about to be signed any moment now," and promised that as soon as he had that fat check in hand, everyone would be paid.

One day, Jerry announced that the startup had acquired two new clients: one in Southern California and one in Seattle. Jerry flew to both locations and delivered the goods, but after he returned from the trips, he didn't mention any payments from clients.

Cameron was getting very stressed out about money, so he sent Jerry a text message asking for the overdue checks. Once again, Jerry promised, "within two weeks." Exasperated, Cameron replied, "We may not last another two weeks." Jerry replied, "Then we will pay for your funerals."

As expected, Jerry lost key members soon after; the startup lost traction and tanked within a year.

The right people are hard to find. You won't know how working with them will turn out until you're together. Consider asking the candidate to perform a trial run or a test project with you to determine if there's a good fit on both sides.

If a candidate doesn't seem suitable, don't hire him/her. Don't settle, because those who aren't aligned with you—in temperament, values, habits, talents, and/or skill sets—may slow you down or derail you.

Startup Anecdotes

Finding the right people is sometimes a matter of being in the right place at the right time. Keeping them is always the result of treating them well and ensuring they are constantly learning, being challenged, and being compensated properly.

Co-founders Dana and Kelly met their future product developer at an entrepreneur's gathering and struck up a conversation. Many meetings ensued regarding skills, purpose, mission, values, and goals. A few weeks later, they hired him, and later two other developers. Service agreements were signed. The small startup team collaborated easily; they exchanged ideas and together built the prototype and later the product.

Dana and Kelly always made time to thank the team members for their resourcefulness and hard work. On the first of each month, Dana would pay everyone promptly. Dana and Kelly were bootstrapping, but they weren't miserly. At holiday times, they treated each team member with a gift certificate to a favorite source of stress relief: massages, exercise gear, and music. They accommodated one of the developers, when his father was dying.

Kelly and Dana succeeded in retaining their team by practicing a core value of their startup: people come first. Inspired by this leadership, their team returned in kind and didn't mind extra time and effort, when needed.

If you find the right people for you, do everything to keep them.

Research and examine the following issues before defining what a "right" employee means to you. Articulate your values, attitudes, hiring criteria, and expectations.

Exercise 43: Examine Your Attitudes and Expectations

1. What is your attitude toward talent management? Do you enjoy managing people? If yes, what do you enjoy about it? If no, what do you find challenging?
2. What value do you place on individual contributions? How do you reward team members? Do you value result and also give credit for effort?
3. Do you want the best talent and are you willing to pay for it? What does "best" mean to you? Best skills? Best personality? Best fit with your team, with venture's culture?

Build Your Internal Team

You are your first hire. Much of this book has focused on your development as a founder. Reflect carefully about what kind of founder you will be because you set the tone for your internal team. If there's one or two things that you want people to associate with you as their leader, what will they be?

Before you hire your next team member, review the following roles and responsibilities, and think about how they fit into the company that you plan to build.

Earlier in the Founder section, I provided a snapshot of basic organization to help you think about various functional roles that you may perform throughout your venture's journey. Review all the positions in the basic organizational structure. Keep them in mind as you create your own team.

Decide Which Hats You Shall Wear

In addition to your founder role, decide which roles you shall assume during the first two years and assess your own qualifications. Identify the roles where you will need help.

Below is a template for you to use and revise as needed.

Exercise 44: Roles You Shall Assume

Startup Roles			
Role	Check which hat(s) you shall wear during first two years	How qualified are you for this position (1 = not very; 2 = competent; 3 = very qualified)	What skills you will need to develop; where will you need support
Founder			
CEO			
President			
CFO			
VP Marketing			
VP Engineering / CTO			
VP Business Development / Sales			
Counsel			
Other			

Thus far, you've reflected, assessed, and articulated your role as founder. You also decided what additional hats to wear during the first two years. And you've identified areas where you may need help.

Say you decide your second hire will be a co-founder to help you start and build the business.

Examine Your Reasons for Hiring a Co-founder

When you start your venture as sole founder, you're responsible for everything. You have complete control over your vision and purpose. You get to define your culture.

When you start your venture with a co-founder, your responsibilities are shared and your decisions require consensus or compromise. You may have two captains at the helm. What are you willing to compromise?

You need to decide when and if it's appropriate to have a co-founder and at what juncture in your journey. Which role(s) will your co-founder assume?

Exercise 45: Reasons for a Co-founder

Reflect carefully and be honest about your reasons. Ask yourself the following:

1. Why do I need a co-founder?
2. What can role that s/he fulfill that I cannot?
3. What will happen if I don't hire a co-founder for the first year? What duties can I assume, if I need to bootstrap?
4. What if I hire a consultant to perform skill sets that I don't have?
5. What compensation package can I afford? How much equity am I willing to give up?
6. Do I need co-founder or do I want one?

Founder Insights

Begin as a founder. Develop and grow into your founder role. Avoid deciding that you need a co-founder just because you feel insecure starting out by yourself. Strive for self-reliance first. Assess yourself and acquire competency in areas where you need it. In a short time—within your first six months or a year—you will know if you need a co-founder to support you. By then, you will have clarity regarding what you need in your co-founder.

Avoid hiring a co-founder first because s/he is a friend, a former colleague, or a relative and then figuring out what you need from this individual. Make this decision based on what your business needs, what you as founder-captain need.

If you're an all-around business person, you may not need a co-founder. If you're a creative and artistic type but you lack business skills and operational experience, you may consider finding someone to help you in these functional areas—but that person doesn't have to become the co-founder.

If you're great in business development, but don't have product development skills, find yourself a qualified product person. Discover if this individual is aligned with you on multiple fronts: personality, values, habits, standards, and communication process. If all your criteria are met, hire the individual for a trial period as a product manager before you offer the co-founder position.

I've worked with dozens of co-founders and founders. Nine out of ten times, people partnered for the wrong reason. Here are two examples.

Startup Anecdotes

A couple decided to start a venture; neither one had worked with the other professionally. Neil and Corey relied on their personal relationship to carry them and so they did not assign their duties formally, detailing who was responsible for what. Nor did they track their performance and progress. Their relationship came first and their new startup came second. Often, when critical business decisions required their attention, they would postpone in favor of solving some crisis from home. They never got any down time because they did not separate home life from work life. The venture's challenges became a 24/7 burden. They were constantly exhausted; they lost perspective. This led them to make some unwise decisions based on fear instead of clear analysis. Their venture folded within 20 months.

•••

In another case, founder Andy decided to enlist one of his best friends to become CEO of his new venture. Andy and Jake had met through a local band and had never worked together. Within six months, it was apparent that Andy, the founder, and his friend Jake, the CEO/Co-founder, did not share the same vision, values, work ethics, and standards. Andy was organized, courteous, and thoughtful. Jake was disorganized, rude, and thoughtless. He didn't value team members as human beings, only as worker bees who were paid to deliver.

Jake and Andy had different ideas about project management and team management. This misalignment created miscommunication, tension, and confusion for the entire startup team. Developers, project managers, designers, and suppliers didn't know if they should take instructions from Andy or from Jake.

Within the first year Jake forced his friend Andy out and took over the startup. The venture failed in the second year because of many reasons, including chaotic project management, and high turnover due to loss of respect for the co-founders. Jake proved to be a poor leader who did not recognize that his venture's best assets were his people. He expected people to be available 24/7 and work long hours, yet was late in paying them. Andy started out with a good community-building idea; he never saw it come to fruition because he hired one of his best friends without assessing the guy through the eyes of a business person.

Often, first-time founders lack the self-confidence to consider starting out with a self-reliant mindset. Too quickly they assume they need a co-founder, so they pick someone they know in order not to go at it alone. They don't assess their co-founder objectively and this action ends up derailing the venture because they are mismatched.

So, you want a co-founder. You're bringing on board someone who is going to be your partner. What determines a good fit for you, for your company? Reflect carefully on the following issues before making your decision.

Exercise 46: Choose a Co-founder

Criteria for a Co-founder			
Factor	Founder	Co-founder / Candidate 1	Identify winning points and potential conflicts
Core Values			
Sources of influence (top 3)			

Criteria for a Co-founder			
Factor	Founder	Co-founder / Candidate 1	Identify winning points and potential conflicts
Habits • General • Mental • Work • Wellness			
Action skills • Initiate • Plan • Execute • Solve • Lead			
Management skills • Self management • Time management • Communications • Relationship management • Project management • Stress management • Crisis management • Financial management			

Criteria for a Co-founder			
Factor	Founder	Co-founder / Candidate 1	Identify winning points and potential conflicts
Other skills			
Industry experience			
Qualities • Self-aware- ness • Self-reliance • Discernment • Adaptability • Steadfastness • Perseverance • Optimism • Empathy			
Other qualities			
Hobbies / Interests			

You may modify this template and use it to assess other candidates.

In the Global Issues section, we focused on your brand identity and cultural norms. If you have a well-articulated brand and culture, it is easier to attract those who find resonance.

We also focused on finding and hiring the right people. Technical and functional skills are important, but don't value these skills over assets such as personality, values, habits, and life goals.

Understand your requirements for each job position. The position requirements may change over time because your startup's needs may change. Recognize that some individuals are good with startup phases, and others are good with operational phases. Someone who is great at creating a product and launching it many not be so great at scaling it. Think ahead.

Be clear about the compensation package and benefits you're offering to the candidates.

In the big picture, it is not necessary that your workers share all your beliefs and values. There are professionals who perform well in spite of the fact that they don't love what they're doing or are mad about the company's products. In the long run, you and your team members will get more out of your collaboration if you all are more aligned on the fundamentals.

Each new team member is an ambassador of your brand. Before your team members interact in their respective roles with your customers and potential partners, they need to acquire an understanding and knowledge of the following:
- Your company's brand identity
- Your culture (values, norms, and performance standards)
- Your product or service (from ideation to getting it in the customer's hands and providing support)
- Your direct and indirect competition
- Your sales and marketing strategies.

Hire the wrong person—someone who doesn't share your values, purpose, goals, and standards; or someone who doesn't care about your brand—and you and your operation will suffer.

A trial period may be a good idea for you and your new team member. Ensure that each individual you bring on board fits in with the community that you're building.

Establish Your External Team

Your external team comprises suppliers, consultants, accountants, bookkeepers, strategic partners, and investors. It is important as your internal team. Think about the kind of suppliers and external partners you want to engage with because the quality of their work will affect what you're producing and selling.

When it comes to vendors and strategic partners, many founders and startup teams didn't have a thorough vetting process. Many were held hostage by the Immediacy Mindset and rushed to the next milestone. They bootstrapped and defaulted to three basic criteria: required functional skills, cheapest services, and fastest delivery.

They didn't verify the candidates' past performances. They didn't make time to understand what vendors valued or standards they had in place. Another error was to rely on friends' or colleagues' recommendations without properly vetting candidates. Many a time, founders engaged contractors, suppliers, vendors to discover half way through a project that they were incompatible on many fronts, such as responsiveness, communication style, and quality of service or materials sold.

Startup Anecdotes

In the late 2000s, I worked with a social networking platform provider who hired technical consultants from a South American country to save money. The South American consultants were competent technically, but not fluent in English, so a lot of time was spent explaining and clarifying our requests. Unlike American clients who expect answers within 24 hours if not before the end of the same business day, our South American peers would answer emails and chats every other day. The result was constant frustration from U.S. clients who expected immediate updates, and headaches for various project managers who had to interact with the South American team. One U.S. client got so frustrated with the slow progress that he fired the startup.

•••

In 2010, I worked with a healthcare startup that hired a local developer who had a team in South Asia. We liked the owner of the firm and we put him through a rigorous hiring process. We checked references and looked at past work. We shared the prototype and product requirements. We were promised a reasonable project plan and time line.

Unfortunately, a huge disconnect existed somewhere between what we communicated to the local developer and what he communicated to his South Asian team of developers. We agreed on a weekly progress review meetings, yet each week, we only received half of what promised, and what was delivered fell way below our expectations, in spite of the fact that we had provided explicit requirements and images of how we wanted our product to appear.

Week after week, our frustration grew as the South Asian team fell further and further behind with their deliverables. The local owner kept apologizing and promising to make things right.

It took us six weeks to conclude that we were never going to get the results we wanted. Essentially, we had wasted almost three months (a month of search and interviews, and almost two months of working with this firm) and had to start anew.

•••

In 2012, I joined a software startup team as product lead. The two co-founders had already hired an engineering firm in San Jose, which outsourced the work to another firm in South Asia. So, in addition to staying up late, working the graveyard shift so we could chat in real time to resolve glitches and clarify our instructions, we also had to deal with language, business, and cultural differences. For some reason, the South Asian developers never completed the daily to-dos as promised, in spite of our repeated requests that the work be done and delivered on time, as promised.

The co-founders were equally frustrated. But they had decided to bootstrap and go with an overseas team that charged them less than a local team. The consequences: wasted time and energy that ended up costing the startup more than what they thought they would save.

Every country has its own business standards and norms. When you hire overseas workers, you need to ensure that they and you come to an understanding about workflow and deliverables. What can you expect from them regarding troubleshooting, problem solving, and response time? And what can they expect from you regarding workflow, dead-lines, response time, and payment processes?

Work with overseas consultants if you have had prior experience and know they are dependable and responsible—and more important, understand your own business culture and work standards. Don't hire people because their services are cheap.

In addition to these three anecdotes, I've been in many other situations where the work was not performed as promised, which resulted in founder frustrations, project delays, and wasteful expenses.

"The right people" also include suppliers, consultants, intellectual property and corporate attorneys, accountants, bookkeepers, strategic partners, and investors. You'll need to spend time vetting your external teams. Develop your criteria for hiring and collaborating with them.

Exercise 47: Initial Due Diligence of Your External Team

Research and learn as much about your consultants, potential partners, and suppliers as possible.

1. What are their professional and educational backgrounds?
2. What kind of projects have they done and what were the outcomes?
3. Who are their current and past clients? Conduct reference checks to verify their work and learn about their performance. How satisfied were the clients?
4. Do your candidates' companies have industry ratings or awards? Better Bureau Business (BBB) ratings?
5. How would you rate their brand? High-end? Low-end?
6. Envision how would collaborating with them affect your venture's brand position, if at all?

Exercise 48: Choose Your Supplier / Strategic Partner

Criteria for Supplier / Strategic Partner	
Criteria	Assess; identify winning points and potential conflicts
Candidate Name / Company Name	
Individual Assessment • Communication process • Responsiveness • Promptness • Humility • Presentation and Execution	
Background (education, profession, and industry)	
Project management standards and processes	
Current and past clients • Project scopes • Project results • Overall performance (responsiveness, promptness, integrity, detail-oriented, and resourcefulness) • Budgets • Client assessments • Industry / BBB rating	
Brand alignment • How would you rate their brand? • How will collaborating them affect your brand?	

Criteria for Supplier / Strategic Partner	
Criteria	Assess. Identify winning points and potential conflicts.
Proposal costs and payment structure • What is the proposed budget to you? • How do they want to be paid?	
Performance metrics (If you plan to hire this person and his/her firm for ongoing work, consider establishing annual performance metrics.)	
Pros (What are this candidate's competitive advantages? What is s/he bringing to the table that is unique and helpful to you and your venture?)	
Cons (What are the trade-offs for you? What quality were you hoping for, but failed to get with this candidate?)	

Use the same process and templates for hiring internal and external team members.

Founder Insights

Check references. Pay attention to what former and current clients say, how they say it, and what they're not saying.

Hiring consultants:
- If you have worked with the individual before, then it's fine to hire him/her and allow this person to work remotely.
- If you have not worked with the overseas consultant before, hire locally.
- Conduct a trial run by providing a small project to determine how well you collaborate and how well the consultant performs.
- Establish frequent touch-base chats/calls. Set milestones. Review performance often.

Sometimes you will come across programmers, technicians, suppliers, or specialists whom you like, but they don't fit for the project that you're trying to complete for reasons of timing, budget, project scope, or skills. Keep in touch with them because they may be a good fit for the next project. It's how I was able to find help for new projects that materialized suddenly because of clients' urgent needs.

Defining what the right people mean to you is the first step toward an effective talent management program that helps you keep them. Now that you have your criteria for them, you also need to ensure the following are in place before you start telling friends and family you're hiring.

If you've not been a hiring manager, acquire basic competency for job postings, interviews, and hiring.

Exercise 49: Talent Management Checklist

1. Acquire knowledge of labor laws and hiring practices.

2. Acquire knowledge of equity compensation structure.

3. Establish your hiring criteria for internal and external teams.

4. Know how to create a job posting. If you've never written a job posting before, check out the postings on Glassdoor or Craig's List, and familiarize yourself with posting format and content. Beyond the job description, experience, and skills required, your posting also reflects your knowledge of employment practices and compensation structure.

5. Once you've posted your opening and received resumes, conduct initial background verification before your interview if possible, otherwise, after interview and before job offer.

6. Prepare for your interviews with your candidates.
   - Decide if you will include both informal and structured interviews.
   - Decide if will you ask the candidates to take competency assessment tests. Who will prepare and administer those tests?
   - Prepare questions you plan to ask and also questions that may be posed to you. As you're creating your job postings, reflect upon your offerings (benefits and trade-offs) to your employees so you can communicate clearly during your interviews. A good question to pose to yourself is why someone would want to work for you.

7. If you have acquired a favorable impression of your candidate, consider offering a trial period for both sides to determine if there's a good fit.

8. Prepare your employment contract template, which should include the following: job description (responsibilities, location, hours, duration), performance (monthly, quarterly, annual) review terms, compensation terms (stock options, profit sharing), benefits (health, holidays, vacation, sick leave), non-disclosure clause, intellectual property rights, and termination.

9. If you plan to hire your new employees as consultants, services such as Nolo offer templates for hiring contractors. You can also find simple service agreement templates online if it's work-for-hire.

10. If you're hiring a full-time employee, consult a corporate attorney specializing in startups to create the appropriate employment contracts.

11. Prepare your Talent Management Guide. All businesses are required to communicate their employment policy to employees. The following information is included in this guide: work hours, work location, dress code requirements, use of equipment guideline, business etiquette, performance metrics, vacation, holiday, sick leave, and other benefits.

12. Plan to conduct performance reviews as scheduled.

All these tasks and measures should be in place by the time your first hire starts. A final insight on finding the right people...

Homogeneity or Difference
Humans are birds of a feather; we flock together. It's understandable to celebrate similarities. It's also important to step out of our comfort zone and collaborate with people of different sensibilities, skills, talents, interests, and backgrounds. Different does not mean incompatible.

Diversity enriches your company's culture and product. Your customers will benefit, and in return, you'll benefit.

We live in a multicultural and multilingual society. Most likely, the product or service you are launching will address customer segments that include both men and women of different age groups, orientations, backgrounds, and geographical locations.

Yet even in our current entrepreneurial landscape, startups comprise all men or all women. Or all company employees come from one distinct segment of age, race or background.

Startup Anecdotes

A company with all men misses a woman's sensibility and perspective, and vice versa. I've worked in projects where I was the lone woman and noticed how men seldom considered how the other half of the human race would respond to male-centric designs and features. I've also worked in female-run projects and noticed how we would have welcomed a man's take on questions we asked and information we delivered. Both companies could have gained from another perspective on form and content.

My friend John, who praised and endorsed diversity, is building a startup with a product for both men and women. John told me he hired more people to support him, so I asked about the gender distribution. He surprised me by saying it was all men. What's remarkable is that John, like many entrepreneurial peers, is creating products for various customer segments, but doesn't have a representation of said segments integrated into his product development and evaluation process.

•••

The 17th century French scholar Henri Estienne wrote, "If youth only knew, if age only could." A startup filled with people in their 20s and 30s is heavy on energy and enthusiasm, and light on experience and wisdom.

In the first dot-com wave, I was one of those young things who didn't quite relate to an older research manager, but appreciated her resourceful approach. A Millennial does not have a Boomer's life experience. On numerous occasions, young founders have told me, "We wished we had known better and hired a seasoned CFO / Bus Dev VP / Marketing VP instead of trying to wing it ourselves." A young regional sales manager for a hip tea company told me that the 20-something founders wasted a lot of time and effort because they didn't have operational, marketing, and talent management experience. I've watched inexperienced entrepreneurs reinvent the wheel because they didn't know better, because they lacked experience. Don't discount "old folks."

On the other hand, a venture filled with people in their 40s and 50s may have abundant wisdom and experience but lack exuberance of youths who are still unscathed by life's experiences and who still ask, "Why?" or expect support with a "Why Not?" Boomers don't have the bottomless energy of Millennials. Recently, a successful career consultant told me that she was very glad she hired a 30-year-old to help her with marketing because of his "Millennial perspective and gung-ho energy." Don't discount "young things."

If you are offering a service to or creating a product for a diverse group of customers, you need to obtain diverse inputs. Step away from your tribe, and be open to people with different world views or ways of doing things. Make sure each hire is a good fit.

•••

In the Global Issues section, you created the DNA that will be present in all aspects of your operation. You thought about your culture and the essential components that will support it. This PEOPLE section addresses how to find the right people to build your team.

The time to reflect, research, and articulate your hiring criteria and process is before you start. Avoid scrambling to fill a position that acquires apparent importance because of the market's sudden demand for your service or goods.

Next, we'll focus on creating an infrastructure that supports both your operation and your product.

Build Your Infrastructure

This section focuses on the infrastructure of an established operation: research, marketing, sales, business law, and finance.

Familiarize yourself with each department's function before you focus time and energy on proving your product idea. Each department is part of your venture's foundation and has an integral role in how you develop your product and run your company.

Avoid mistakes committed by many first-time founders. They often: 1) think that all they need is a great idea and time to develop their product, 2) avoid developing areas where they feel intimidated because of lack of competency, and 3) hire someone else to handle what they avoid and remain uninformed.

Great product development—whether physical or a service—isn't something that stands alone. It requires research, reflection, and incorporation of other integral elements to support it, like brand identity, marketing, pricing, distribution, customer service, and sales.

Before you focus on your product, build infrastructure to support its growth. Ignoring critical areas that are integral to your operation will cause disaster.

Founder Insights

You don't need to be expert in all departments. As founder, you possess unique competencies. Leverage areas where you're most competent and spend time developing what needs strengthening. The more you know about all aspects of your operation, the more influence, power, and control you will have over its direction.

Research

Research usually falls to the Marketing department. Think of Research as an ongoing task that extends beyond marketing or R&D responsibility. All your crew should wear a Research hat at all times.

You'll need two kinds of research: market and consumer. You'll want to learn as much as you can about the business landscape you plan to enter.

Exercise 50: Market Research

Market Size and Penetration Rate
Market penetration is the sales volume of goods or services compared to the total target market for that product or service.[16]
- Is your product or service in a new, growing, or mature niche?
- What is the industry size and market penetration rate, if this is not a new product or service?
- What is the niche market size and what is its penetration rate?
- What are the easiest entry points? What are the obstacles?
- What are the industry's and market niche's annual sales and profit margins?

If you're entering an existing market, you'll have more market data at your disposal and often, higher entrance barriers. If research reveals that entry barriers are high because of saturation, regulation, or high overhead, you may want to reconsider your business idea.

If you're creating a new niche with few markers, you'll need to focus on consumer and product testing to gauge consumer interest.

Market Trends
- What trends are driving current markets?
- What are the current legislation or local ordinances that will influence your new business operation and expenditures?
- What about political changes, environmental, socioeconomic, and/or cultural shifts? Will these affect demand for your new product idea?
- What other related industry changes may affect your business path in one year, in five years?
- How will technology aid or render obsolete what you plan to do?

Competitive Analysis
Competitive analysis is a must, because it influences the future of your business. Here are key questions you need to address:
- Will the product create a new market or will it fall into existing one?
- Has anyone created a similar product or service? Research intellectual property issues.
- Let's say Company A and Company B create a similar product to what you have in mind.
  - Are their brand strategies and messaging similar to yours? If so, what are the similarities and differences? How can you stand out?
  - Are their customers your targeted customers?

- Who are your direct competitors and industry's leaders?
  - What are their market shares?
  - What are their current competitive advantages?
  - What are their Achilles' heels?
  - Are there underdogs? Why?
  - What are the entry barriers, if any?
- Who are your indirect competitors?
  - How could they dislodge you? For example, if you're planning to sell sausages, you're competing directly with other sausage and hot dog vendors. Your indirect competitors would be sandwich, burger, taco, and pizza vendors.
  - How may you dislodge them?

You'll need to perform an analysis showing how your venture would stack up against your competitors. Below is a template to get you started. You'll need to customize to fit your needs and industry.

Exercise 51: Assess Competition

Competitive Research				
Factor	Your business	Competitor A	Competitor B	Comments
Company name				
Team • Experience • Talents • Skills				
Brand • Reputation • Quality • Loyalty • Unique selling point				

Competitive Research				
Factor	Your business	Competitor A	Competitor B	Comments
Product • R&D • Appearance • Performance • Scalability				
Packaging				
Distribution				
Pricing				
Promotion				
Public Relations				
Location and size				
Customer profile				
Customer service				
Market share				
Annual revenues				
Annual growth rate				
Budget size				
Access to financial support for additional R&D				

Consider including direct competitors, indirect competitors, and potential competitors.

Consumer Research
In addition to market research, you'll need consumer research. Build your customer profile by asking the following.

Exercise 52: Consumer Research

Who is your ideal customer? Perhaps you have more than one target audience.

1. What are your customer segments and how do these factors matter?
   • Demographics (age, income, education, etc.)
   • Psychographics
          (personalities, values, lifestyles, interests, etc.)
   • Behavioral (purchasing patterns and habits)
   • Geographics
          (neighborhoods, zip codes, cities, counties, states, etc.)

2. Who are the decision makers and buyers?

3. Where and when will they buy your product / service? Is this a one-time or recurring purchase?

4. How much will they pay?

•••

If you have more than one segment, prioritize and develop one at a time.

These are initial research steps; you take them to prepare for your venture. You'll need ongoing in-depth research as you proceed. Your target segment(s) may change with new information and insights.

Founder Insights

When you're starting out, your first customer(s) may or may not be your ideal customer(s). Necessity may compel you to take on these initial customers, but don't be beholden to them. Don't compromise your values and standards.

A good customer is one who is happy with your product (or service) and pays on time. An excellent customer is one who is happy with your product, pays you promptly, gives you constructive feedback, and recommends your product to others.

As you acquire more customers, you may find that your initial customers may or may not be your targeted customers. You'll need to adjust whatever customer segment and business model (product revision, channel revision, etc.) you have in mind as you move along.

Incorporate all the market and consumer research that you've conducted thus far into your marketing strategy.

Marketing

In an established and successful company, a marketing department operates with its essential components integrated and synchronized.

If you're unfamiliar with marketing, here's a summary. Established companies employ the traditional four Ps (product, price, promotion, and place / distribution) as their marketing mix. Its origins can be traced back to a Harvard Professor named James Culliton, who published an article about marketers and "mixers of ingredients" in 1948. In 1960, E. Jerome McCarthy wrote a book on marketing and formally adopted the four Ps as a marketing framework for businesses.

In the 1980s, Bernard H. Booms and Mary J. Bitners included physical evidence, people, and process—expanding the marketing mix to seven. In 1990, Robert F. Lauterborn proposed a new classification of marketing mix to replace traditional 4Ps.[17] This mix included consumer (wants and needs), cost, communication, and convenience. Keep these components in mind as you're planning your marketing strategy.

In the current startup landscape, new entrepreneurs follow the herd and begin by focusing solely on product development. First, your product can't thrive or survive without a marketing strategy and delivery system in place. Second, when and how you start thinking about your marketing department will impact your operation. If you begin by focusing exclusively on product and delaying research on distribution, promotion, pricing, and packaging until you're ready to showcase your prototype, you will find yourself backtracking to incorporate essential marketing elements into your creation.

Founder Insights

View marketing as an umbrella that covers its integral components, and approach product development systemically. This mindset keeps essential components up front as you build product.

Acquire operational knowledge in product, distribution, promotion, and pricing. If your product is a physical one and requires packaging, include this in your mix. Each component should have a strategy that integrates with overall strategy. Each should reflect the company's brand strategy.

Marketing > Product
Product is the first element that founders address. The next section focuses on product and, in particular, developing proof of concept to determine whether your idea is worth pursuing.

Marketing > Distribution
If you're not familiar with distribution, you'll need to conduct research. Basic distribution questions you need to answer in your initial phase:

- Is your business a brick and mortar business, an omni-channel retailer (online and retail), or an online store? Will you sell exclusively in physical or online stores?
- Will you rely on Amazon, eBay, and/or other affiliate marketers? These may charge you a promotion fee, sometimes called a "slotting fee" or affiliate marketing fee.
- What distribution channels will you employ? You'll need to research channels that are appropriate for your product, as well as costs for doing business with these distributors.

You'll need to research how competitors distribute products and how wholesalers, retailers, and agents operate.

Once you've researched them, choose one or two that you believe will be most effective for your business model. Test one or two distribution channels with a trial run.

Marketing > Promotion
There are two types of promotion: consumer and trade. Consumer promotion provides consumers with incentives to purchase, such as a coupon, special offer, or reward program. Trade promotion provides incentives to distributors, sales teams, and brokers to enlist their support and endorsement of your product.

You can promote your product—through public relations, traditional channels (print, radio, and TV), direct sales, word-of-mouth, and social media (networks, forums, media sharing, blogs, microblogs, and podcasts). You'll need to research to determine the most appropriate forms to promote your product. Test a channel's effectiveness by conducting trials.

Marketing > Pricing

Of marketing components, pricing is one of the more difficult, especially if you're creating something new that has no direct competition. If you lack experience in pricing strategy and analysis, research (online and offline) how companies price products in similar niches.

Founder Insights

What is the right price? Pricing something new is complicated. If you're creating a new market without direct competitors, test your potential customer base; highlight your product's unique features and competitive edge, and ask what you want customers to pay. Be realistic. If there's repeated resistance (no buyers), then adjust your price and see what people are willing to pay, not what you want them to pay. You might add value to your product or service, and then ask for what you want to be paid.

If entering a market thick with other players, you can price your product competitively and promote distinguishing features.

You can start with a lower price, but if you start out at the bottom, you have no place to go. Once people associate your business with providing "cheap or value-laden" products or services, you'll have difficulty changing your brand's reputation. If you base your business model on offering the cheapest, someone may lower price further. This isn't a winning proposition long-term.

•••

Uniqlo, a well-known Japanese clothing brand for young adults, started with low pricing and got stuck with it. Customers were so used to its low price points that when Uniqlo tried to raise prices 5% in 2014 and followed up with a 10% hike in 2015, their retail store traffic dropped 6% during a six-month period.[18] Uniqlo restored old prices.

•••

Some new businesses employ a "freemium" strategy, where customers use the basic product free, until they add features or services; then they're charged a premium.

Many startups never generate customers and fail. The freemium model brings down a new company's value from the start. Today, most of the "free" products or services aren't really "free;" they have strings attached. The "free" version gets customers hooked; then they have to pay to upgrade. Or it may be free, but customers must agree to allow their information to be shared with other marketers.

Offering your product as a freemium will dilute your brand's position. If you have an innovative or outstanding business idea, allow it to stand on its own. Do not diminish its worth by giving it out to anyone who's willing to take it. What has no price is worth nothing.

If you want to offer freemiums, prepare to become an advertising channel because that is how you will pay your bills. This defeats the purpose of starting your venture in the first place—selling your product that you believe in and making it a success. The freemium strategy should never be your first choice.

Here's a list of question to help you with your initial pricing plan.

Exercise 53: Pricing

Pricing Checklist
1. How much does it cost to create a prototype? A full product?
2. What will be your fixed and variable costs? Are there economies of scale?
3. What's the production cost, using the lowest cost method?
4. What is your pricing model? Realize that you'll be going through multiple revisions.
5. How much will you charge for the product?
6. Are there different price points—depending on different distribution channels?
7. Is your price point competitive?
8. How much does it cost for you to acquire a customer?
9. What is your break-event point? (Break-even: you're generating enough revenues to cover expenses, while making neither a profit nor a loss.)
10. What is your profitability point? (Profitability: what is left after you've used revenues to pay operating expenses.)
11. What are your forecasts?

A reality check. How much it would cost you to acquire your first customer, your 10th customer, and your 100th customer? Will what you charge cover costs and generate profit? Where will your operation break even? When will it generate a profit?

Marketing > Packaging

In addition to the traditional four Ps, there's packaging. If your product is physical and requires packaging, you'll need to understand your target customer segments and their purchasing preferences, including the kind of packaged products that they often purchase.

You'll also need to research packaging elements, which include product protection appearance, composition (eco-friendly), design, function, manufacturing, and disposal. And you'll need to vet packaging vendors on manufacturing capabilities, logistics, support, pricing, overall performance, and reputation. The latter includes how eco-friendly they are.

Address all marketing components—product, distribution, promotion, pricing, and packaging—as an integrated system. Research and study the areas where you've little knowledge to acquire competence. Ensure your marketing plans reflect your brand strategy.

Sales

You may have something great to sell, but if you can't convince customers to buy it, you'll run aground. You need someone good at selling.

When starting out and bootstrapping, selling product starts with the founder. If you possess clarity and conviction in product ideas and are passionate about sharing it, you're selling. You sell your product idea to your partner to obtain support to start a venture. You sell your idea to friends and family to raise seed money. You sell to potential collaborators to enlist their help. Selling never ends.

If you don't have a sales background, read books about it. Interview colleagues with business development skills to pick up a few tips. Your "founding" team members need to possess basic sales skills, too. Don't wait until you're able to hire a VP of Sales.

Startup Anecdotes

A common mistake that first-time founders commit is to hire a salesperson and set this person loose without communicating to him/her their branding position, and providing training and sales tools.

A second mistake is not recognizing the need to establish a "handing-off" process from sales manager, who gets the Service Agreement or Work Order signed by the customer, to account manager, who handles post-sale activities.

I've witnessed sales managers who over-promised to clients and failed to communicate this to account managers, who were left on the receiving end of client frustration when fulfillment failed or were beyond the project's scope. I've witnessed account managers who deliberately kept sales managers out of the product update loop by not sharing product updates.

Founders need to connect the sales team with account managers and the product team. Founders should require transparency in communication and establish accountability for all involved.

What do you need to create for your Sales department?

Exercise 54: Sales

Sales Checklist
1. Your brand identity and position are in place—you've completed branding exercises and are clear about what your company represents—and you've communicated that to all your team members, including new Sales hires.
2. Your basic marketing collateral and sales tools (which reflect your brand) are ready.
3. Your company's sales pitch needs is developed (and refined over time).
4. An agreement on pricing structures, commission and reward structures, a Sales / Service Agreement draft, and a post-sales support process are in place before your sales team heads out the door.

Business Law
Here we focus on additional business and legal issues that you'll need to research and address before embarking on your venture. Many first-time founders find this intimidating because of lack of knowledge.

You'll empower yourself and increase your value as a founder when you show potential new hires that you know what you have to offer. You'll find books and online resources about doing business in your state, such as your local chamber of commerce and state government's websites.

Conduct research and set up your structure and process properly. Many tasks can be completed without a corporate attorney, such as business name and domain name registration, incorporation, and insurance. You'll need legal help for patents and other intellectual properties rights, and structuring equity offerings for new hires or investors.

Business Name and Registration
What is your business name? What is your domain name? You may learn more about business name and registration your city government's website. Your domain name should mirror your business name. You may search for domain name availability at any of the established domain registrars such as GoDaddy or Network Solutions.

In the first dot-com wave, businesses snapped up the most memorable and succinct names. The rest of the world was left with few options. New entrepreneurs started using compound words and making up new names. In our global markets, you'll need to test what your venture's name means and how it sounds in other languages. Make sure it is easy to spell, pronounce, and remember.

Incorporation / Business Structure
Decide what business entity your startup will assume: sole proprietorship, partnership, limited partnership, C corporation, or S corporation. You may find filing information and cost of incorporation at your city's and state government's websites.

Ownership

Will you run your business as an individual proprietorship or look for co-founders? If the latter, you'll need to know about equity structure, shareholder's rights, transfer of ownership, and vesting process. Most important, you'll need to know about these issues before you interview, make an offer, and hire your second employee.

Founder Insights

Equity allotments to new employees vary among companies and industries. My informal survey among entrepreneurs I know from diverse industries indicates there are no common cross-industry practices. Founders allocate equity portion based on what they want to offer, what they think the candidate is worth, and what the candidate negotiates.

That said, it is common for founders frequently allocate up to 25 percent of their equity for friends and family investors, and first round of new hires. A first new hire receives between 1.5% to 2% of equity and some form of cash. The equity percentage for each new hire also depends on how much cash founders are willing to compensate upfront. Most startups require employees work four years before vesting 100% of their shares. If you are adding two co-founders, each should have the same vesting schedule.

Spend time preparing an Agreement that includes the following:
- Detailed responsibilities and milestones
- Compensation structure (cash, equity structure, vesting period, 83(b) Election))
- Intellectual property that includes a Proprietary Information Agreement Plan (PIAP)
- Company policy and standards (work location, hours, dress code, vacation, sick leave, etc.)

> This way, you will avoid a messy hiring process when find yourself with the sudden need to add new headcount.
>
> When people start working for you and know exactly what they can expect in return, they're more likely start with goodwill and best intentions to perform well for you.

Investors

If you plan to raise money, you'll need to research financing as well as the different types of investor profiles, criteria, and investment models. Common financing sources:

- Personal savings, credit cards
- Friends and family loans (Under $100K)
- SBA loans
- Bank / credit union loans
- Crowd sourcing
- Angel investors ($100K-$200K)
- Venture capitalists ($1M+)

If you want complete ownership and control of your operation for as long as possible, use your own money and bootstrap until you're profitable. If you plan to use other people's money, here's a checklist to consider.

Exercise 55: Checklist for Seeking Capital

When you're ready to seek capital:

- You have all the key team members in place to run a tight and efficient ship.
- Your product is selling.
- You feel confident about your chosen customer segments.
- You're acquiring customers faster than you're able to support them.

- You have garnered substantial paid customers for at least one to two years. You're breaking even and you're on track to making profits. Better yet, you're making profits and you're anticipating an upward trajectory. You have a solid base for creating your financial projections for at least the next two to three years.
- You have an expansion plan for the next two to three years.
- You know why you need to raise money.
- You know how much money you need to raise and how much equity you're willing to give up.
- You know what kind of investors you want: a passive one who'll leave you alone to operate your business, or an active one who can provide ongoing advice and support.

Next, conduct due diligence on the potential investors. Make sure you investigate a few potential candidates so you can compare and have perspective.

- Research their general professional backgrounds. Do they have finance backgrounds? Have they worked for large or small companies? Do they have startup experience? Founder experience?
- What are their industry niches? Do they align with yours? Avoid contacting those who specialize and are not in your category because they won't be interested in talking with you.
- Where did they study and live? Do they have regional and/or international experiences? What are their life experiences?
- What are their investment philosophy and criteria? What companies are in their portfolio? What kind of founders lead these portfolio companies? How have they performed?
- Where do you find resonance and where do you have questions or concerns?

Decide if the potential investors are aligned with your venture's purpose and direction, if they are the kind of people you want to support you and collaborate with you.

Answers to these questions can help you understand the individuals whose money will be used by you. Each time you bring another element (investor) on board, you will have less control, and how you run your ship will change. Some may want to give you money in return for a passive role. Other investors will want to install someone of their own on your executive team, if they don't have full confidence in you and your crew. Consider carefully before you make these changes.

If you live in a metropolitan area, you'll find many founders and entrepreneurs at startup meetups, pitches, and conferences. Tap into your special-interest communities, like arts and crafts, reading, cycling, running, soccer, choir, wine club, church, or temple. Your local alumni club and organizations where you volunteer could also be useful.

Founder Insights

Getting investors to give you money always takes longer than you think. Double or triple the time that you think it will take to receive that check from your new investors. Even if you're operating efficiently and are ready to provide whatever documentation or analysis requested by potential investors, you still have an unknown variable: the person who's writing the check. Make sure you're covered financially while you're presenting, pitching, and convincing.

Bootstrap and avoid giving away equity. Understand that you'll give away a bit more ownership with each new financing round. Don't seek out investment unless you truly need it. Avoid deciding when desperate.

Investors will assess you throughout your venture. Are you great at launching a new business? Are you skilled at running it and expanding it? You've performed well with a crew of ten. Will you perform well with a crew of a hundred? A thousand? The larger your appetite, the more prepared you need to be to scale up successfully.

Not all founders possess startup, growth and expansion skills. Reflect and plan ahead to acquire or refine needed skills for your next operating phase. Don't be sidelined by investors who don't believe in your ability to take the "next" step.

When seeking capital, you'll have more negotiating power if you have an established client base, a steady revenue stream, and expanding markets. Don't waste time chasing investors until you do. Even if you find someone willing to invest, you'll get less money and give away more equity if you haven't a solid financial position.

When you approach potential investors, believe that you have something they want, not as someone eager to sell.

Before you meet potential investors, create a polished presentation. Prepare Frequently Asked Questions (FAQ) and answers. What's in the presentation? Appearance, delivery, and even your pitch matter because they send subliminal messages. As founder, you need to show you're in complete control of your ship.

Plan so that it will be a long time before you need to seek capital. Here's a template of issues you need to research, plan, and include in your Investment Deck—what you present to investors.

Exercise 56: Sample Investment Deck

Investment Deck

1. Executive Summary
   - Product description
   - Product launch and results
   - Customer profile(s)
   - Market opportunity, current and projected revenues
   - Amount of capital sought

2. Market Opportunity

3. Product Overview
   - Feature and functionality
   - Benefits

4. Product Opportunities
   - Proof of concept
   - Markets
   - Channels

5. Competitive Advantages
   - Intellectual property (patents, trademarks, and service marks)
   - Unique features and benefits

6. Value Proposition
   - Team experience
   - Proven product success
   - Proven revenue generation and measurable Return on Investment (ROI)

7. Competition

Investment Deck
8. Risk factors (and mitigation strategy)
9. Finance (performance and projections)
10. Management Team
11. Execution Plan
12. Summary

Presentation is everything. Tell a good story that evokes emotional response. How is your story compelling? Will it prompt your audience to action?

You may develop the most value-laden investment deck, but if your delivery is all facts and no emotion, you might as well not bother. Practice your delivery in front of a mirror. Better yet, film yourself, so you can see how you appear, how you present. If you can, work with a presentation or voice coach. Be prepared to answer what you think will be asked.

Intellectual Property

Domain names, company name and slogan, service mark, trademark, copyright, patent, and licensing agreements are assets and may be mentioned as competitive advantages and value propositions.

What do you need to do to protect intellectual property? What's the process for registration, for filing? What are costs? A good source is U.S. Office of Patent and Trademark. Verify and protect your creation.

Insurance

Business insurance protect your venture from loss, such as employee injury, operational mishaps, or natural disaster that causes equipment or property damage. Learn more about insurance requirements for employers, as well as different types of business insurance. The SBA website provides basics.

Privacy

Company and consumer privacy should be a part of your business strategy. Know about privacy laws; the SBA and the U.S. General Services Administration websites are resources for this.

Contracts

As you engage consultants, vendors, and suppliers, you'll need a basic service agreement. Learn about contract law basics at Nolo or FindLaw before you talk to a corporate attorney. Unless you're trained as a corporate attorney, you should seek the help of one, when offering new hires with a compensation package that includes both cash and equity.

Here is a checklist of issues and areas that you need to research. The deeper your knowledge is, the better.

Exercise 57: Business Law Checklist

Business Law Checklist
1. Business name and registration
2. Incorporation / business structure
3. Intellectual property
4. Privacy
5. Compensation and ownership
6. Insurance
7. Contracts
8. Investors

Finance

As founder, you're in charge of finances. If you've dealt with budgets and financial management, you have a head start. If you haven't, you'll need to assume this role during your initial phase. Start out right; establish your financial footing. Teach yourself basic accounting so you'll know how to plan, manage, and track your business' financial performance.

As you conduct research on costs and prepare your budget, revisit issues below from the Introspection exercises. Keep them fresh in mind.

Exercise 58: Plan Your Finances

Finance Checklist
1. How much money have you saved?
2. How much money will you set aside and not touch, under ANY circumstances?
3. How much money do you need to cover monthly basic needs while you work on the venture?
4. How much money will you invest to start your venture?
5. Will you invest to keep it going until break-even or profitable stage?
6. At what point will you stop funding the venture if it keeps losing money?
7. How much money will you allocate for emergency needs?
8. At what point do you want to raise money, if at all?
9. If you want to raise money, how much do you plan to raise?
10. And how will you use the proceeds?
11. How much control of the company do you plan to keep?
12. When do you expect to see a return on your investment?
13. When do you expect to start saving again?

In the previous section, you reviewed your financial habits and started your financial preparation.

How will you finance your venture? Research your options thoroughly.
- Your own money
- Friends and Family
- Bank / Credit Union / SBA loans
- Angel investors
- Crowd sourcing
- Some combination _____

Founder Insights

Create a separate credit and debit account for seed money. Avoid using your personal bank account for your venture's expenses.

If you bootstrap, track your activity using Excel or QuickBooks. If you can afford it, hire a bookkeeper to set up your accounting system properly.

Doing business always takes more time and money than what you budget. Double your expense allocation.

You'll go through many budget drafts as you acquire more knowledge from your research.

Create Your Budgets

Test before you launch a full-scale venture. Create a Prototype Budget to track your initial expenses. You can fold this budget into your Startup Budget.

Prototype Budget

What does it cost to create a functional prototype? What does it cost to sell it to your first customers?

Each Prototype Budget is unique because it depends on the product or service that you provide. If it involves cooking and selling specialty foods, the prototype costs will be significantly less than if you're planning to create an energy-saving machine that requires significant human resources, material, and manufacturing costs.

Exercise 59: Prototype Budget

Prototype Budget			
Item	Estimated cost	Actual cost	Assess
Concept research and design			
Market research (marketing and consumer research, intellectual property filings, competitive research)			
Prototype production (raw materials, equipment, manufacturing, packaging, recycling costs)			
Initial advertising costs			

Prototype Budget			
Item	Estimated cost	Actual cost	Assess
Human talent (You, designer, engineers, consultants)			
Other costs (travel, communications, foods. etc.)			

Startup Budget

A startup budget should include all Prototype Development costs, as well as other one-time and recurring fees that you'll need for operation in initial years.

Below is a sample budget. List all the cost components, which may include business registration fee, domain registration fee, incorporation fee, brand identity development cost, office supplies, equipment, rent, insurance, website hosting account, website development cost, app development cost, research costs, product development budget, marketing costs (collateral, location fees, packaging, etc.), sales training costs, corporate attorney's fees, bookkeeper's fees, consultants' fees, and travel costs. This sample assumes, as No. One Hire, you're not paying yourself.

Exercise 60: Startup Budget

Startup Budget					
Expense	Estimated cost	Actual cost	One-time or Recurrent	Year 1	Assess
Business registration					
Domain registration					
Incorpora-tion					
Brand identity development					
Research					
Intellectual property filing					
Prototype development					
Full product development (itemized)					
Marketing					
Sales tool / training					
No. 2 hire					
No. 3 hire					
Legal					
Insurance					
Consultants					

Startup Budget					
Expense	Estimated cost	Actual cost	One-time or Recurrent	Year 1	Assess
Meetings / travel / meals					
Administrative					
Misc.					

Set Financial Goals

Once you've researched, figured out expenses, acquired customers, and have a steady revenue stream, set some goals.

Exercise 61: Set Goals

1. What are your annual revenue goals for your new business?

2. How do you define your venture's success? What is your ultimate goal for it?
    *   Money? How much?
    *   Geographical reach? How extensive?
    *   Reputation? How extensive?
    *   Other reason _____

3. Do you have an exit strategy?
    *   Build and run it until you retire.
    *   Build and run it until you've made X profit and sell.
    *   Build and run it until you're bored.
    *   Build to flip.

4. Stay focused on your goals and create an action plan to achieve them.

Manage Your Finances

You will be responsible for finances, even after you hire someone to manage them. Track all expenses and revenues. Again, if you have never managed an operation, read a few books, take an online class, or teach yourself. Acquire accounting knowledge before starting your venture.

•••

The Operation Section should give you a good idea of what you need to do in your Founder role. When you start as a team of one, it's easy to manage yourself, especially if you're an organized individual. As you bring more team members on board, you need to set up the infrastructure to manage your business, your team, and your product.

Before starting out, it's best to research and address your "global" issues, find the right people, and establish the structure needed for both your product and your operation. Don't wait until you're in a hiring frenzy to set up managing criteria.

As founder, you don't need to be an expert in all areas. You do need basic competency in all areas, so that you can perform emergency service. If you know what you need to do in order to attend to your Founder responsibilities, you should be in a better position to add your Product Developer responsibilities. You know it's prudent to test your product idea first with a prototype and trial run.

The Product Section

You've come up with an idea and want to create a prototype to test it. Before expending energy on it, spending some time on this Product Section. It has a Product Definition Exercise and Initial Product Development Plan (PDP). This will help you move forward with focus and clarity. Note that the Exercise is an integral component of the Plan.

Product Definition

Below are 12 essential questions you need to explore and answer.

Exercise 62: Product Definition Exercise

1. What is your product offering?

You'll need to answer this question with confidence and conviction. If you find yourself struggling for an answer, you need to keep researching and refining until you have a succinct and convincing answer. You need to distill this answer to one sentence. Be prepared for questions that follow.

Example: My company offers a _____ service / product to _____ (type of customer) in _____ (online / offline market / industry niche at _____ pricing level.

2. Product Specifications

If your product is a new sandwich, what is the recipe? If your product is a special phone for the elderly, what are its specifications? How user-friendly are its features? If your product is a service that you want to offer, what's the customer's experience?

3. Appearance
   • Features: what does it possess if it's a physical product? What does it smell like? What does it feel like?
   • Functionalities: how is it engineered? How does it work?

4. Appeal
   • How would you describe the product's personality? Does it mirror your company brand's personality?
   • What sets your product apart? What's most memorable in the customer's mind?
   • What emotion does your product or service evoke in the customer?

5. Benefits
- How does it entertain, solve a problem, and/or aid the buyer?
- Does it address a need (solve a problem) or a want?

6. Experience
- What is the customer's experience when using it?

7. Positioning
- How will you get your product in front of your customers?
- If your product is physical, where will you display it in the store? Where will you place it on your website and on your affiliate marketers' websites?
- If your product is a service, how will you educate your customers so they will know what to expect?
- Is your product competing directly with another for the same customers? Is it competing indirectly?
- Is your product targeting a saturated, underserved, or new market?

8. Application.

    Does your product have more than one application? Say you created a product that serves as both umbrella and rain water collector for campers. How will you decide which feature to market first? What criteria will you use: low barrier-to-market entry but a small group of users, or high barrier entry with a large market segment?

9. Will the product create repeat purchases, or is it one-time acquisition?

10. A SWOT Analysis

    Conduct a SWOT test to assess your product idea by looking at Strengths, Weaknesses, Opportunities, and Threats. You'll need this in addition to a competitive analysis. If you're honest with your answers, SWOT analysis will give you a realistic perspective of your product's viability.

Strengths and Weaknesses Analysis (SWOT)

Strengths	Weaknesses
Opportunities	Threats

11. Blind Spot(s)

To identify your product's blind spot(s), ask, "What's the customer's pain?" You've been envisioning how your customer would enjoy your product; now imagine how s/he'd find it cumbersome, time consuming, or difficult to use.

12. 360-degree Assessment

Perform a 360-degree product assessment. Look at your product from different perspectives:

- Your perspective as product creator and founder - What do you believe you're providing to the marketplace, to targeted customer segments? Articulate your value and contribution.

- Your customers' perspective - What are your customers' reactions to your brand presentation and product idea? What do they think you're offering? If it's a competing product, will they see its differentiating qualities?

- Your competitors' perspective - How will they respond to your product? Will they consider you a worthy competitor and up their game? Will your product compel them to innovate? If they have deeper pockets than you, will their innovation wipe out your competitive edge? Will their innovation render yours obsolete?

- The market's perspective - How does your product fit its market? What impact will it make? Does it create ripples in a small pond or a tsunami?

- The technological perspective - How much does your product depend on technology and how much on human resources? The more "automated" your process, the more dependent your business will be on technology. Technology may enable its speedy creation and delivery, but it may hinder you if required hardware and software are costly and execution is cumbersome.

- The eco-friendly perspective - This element may not be a part of your overall brand identity. If it is, does your product require packaging? If so, what kind of cost-efficient materials will you use? Are they toxin-free? Will they be recyclable or will they end up on landfills? If recyclable, are there costs that you can recover, such as paper or metallic elements? The eco-friendly outlook can be as extensive or as limited as you want to be.

- Product and venture alignment - Your original product idea will evolve during research and development. It may change again after you've introduced it to initial users. It may adapt to changing customer tastes. Review its current purpose and core values. How far have you come? Is your current iteration still aligned with your original one?

Give yourself some time to research, reflect, define, and develop your product.

Startup Anecdotes

No one has a monopoly on an idea. Your product may be first to appear, but this does not guarantee success in the intermediate or long term.

Charles Darwin and Alfred Russell Wallace each came up with the theory about natural selection. Darwin published *On the Origin of Species* while Wallace shunned the limelight.[20] Alexander Graham Bell is linked to the telephone. Yet during his time, a controversy occurred over who should receive credit—Bell or Elisha Gray, since both filed patents on the same day.[21]

•••

In the early 2000s, one could find over 35 companies in the social networking platform business. I worked for one. Startup SWFT garnered paying customers and received a few rounds of financing. It never took off because of an absentee CEO, lack of a strong brand, lack of systems and processes, poor quality control, immature engineers, and incompetent sales managers. I recently looked at this list of companies. Most have failed. A few were acquired by competitors.

•••

Long before Google Street View, a talented engineer came up with this idea, created software, and embedded it in a camera, which he built. He placed it on top of his car and drove around San Francisco to capture street views. He enlisted engineers for product development. The startup didn't get far because the founder was focused on refining the product and not on creating a company, which needed people to support him.

In 2007, a startup created Circles, an interest-based social network. This was before Google introduced Google+.

Circles was launched successfully, but it did not flourish because the CEO who headed this and other networking products was a man who loved to listen to his own voice and no one else. Jay ignored all kinds of advice and alerts—regarding functionality, appearance, and user experience—from both his engineers and users. He was also a spendthrift, squandering the money raised to build a poorly functional network that tanked.

So, more than one individual will come up with the same great idea. Yet a great idea that is poorly executed by its founder (and founding team) will fail. You may or may not be the only person who's ever come up with your product idea. What's more important is that you feel compelled to develop it, and that you will focus on the execution part, and not rely on selling the idea itself. It remains an idea and has no value until you turn it into a reality—a well executed one.

Founder Insights

If you have a vision of offering multiple products or services, scale back, and focus on developing one at a time. Research and decide which will be your flagship product. Hint: avoid picking the most complicated product. Start with a simple idea and process. Then focus on developing it, testing it, and rolling it out successfully. Don't dilute your efforts on a few products because you will end up with mediocre things and no clear winner.

Startup Anecdotes

I once worked with two co-founders whose vision included launching a new business with four services. Through the branding exercises and an elimination process, I helped them focus on the flagship product, which possessed the most competitive edge and potential for commercial success. I was gratified when they acknowledged soon after that they had made the right decision. They built the product and launched it successfully.

Now that you've completed your Product Definition exercise, proceed to the Product Development Plan.

Exercise 63: Initial Product Development Plan

The goal is to gather resources and get started. Your plan comprises the following components. Note that you've just completed first one, Product Definition.

1. Product Definition *
You will need to spend some time researching, articulating, and refining your product definition.
   • Features
   • Requirements
* See preceding exercise on Product Definition.

2. Resources
   • Raw materials
   • Equipment (tools and machinery)
   • Human resources: yourself, your employees, and consultants

3. Project Plan
Your plan needs a lead product manager, preferably one who also excels at project management.
- Lead project manager
- Tasks assigned
- Resources allocated
- Timeline (milestones and launch dates)
- Performance review

4. Budget
In the previous Finance section, you've mulled over how you will establish a financial strategy for yourself and your venture. As you proceed, remember that tracking expenses and revenues is essential. And bootstrap.

5. Integration
As you're developing your product, you will need to think about related components: packaging, place / distribution, promotion, and pricing. One of the major mistakes that unseasoned entrepreneurs commit is waiting until after the prototype is developed to incorporate these components. Weave them and your brand into your product as you move forward.

6. Strategy, Goals, and Beyond Your First Two Years
Research, define, and establish your strategy and goals:
- What kind of business model are you pursuing? Build to flip? Build to expand?
- What do you need to validate your first flagship product? Is it the first 100,000 buyers, the first $1M in revenues, and/or the first industry award?
- Once you've achieved Phase I, do you have enough cash flow to build out Phase II?
- What kind of value is your company continuing to create?

As you're implementing Phase I, you need to think of your journey beyond this milestone.

Founder Insights

When you're going through your product-testing phase, take time to assess both positive and negative feedback. Why is your audience so enthusiastic? Or why do they have reservations? Do they provide a reasonable perspective?

Look beyond the enthusiasm and the criticism. Who's providing the feedback? How are their backgrounds influencing their responses? Asking the wrong people (who are not your targeted users) will produce irrelevant feedback at best, or derail you at worst.

Create a weekly, monthly, quarterly, and annual road map. Include goals, milestones, lessons learned, and performance reviews.

CHAPTER RECAP

In this second part of your manifest, the Startup section helped you address three essential areas that affect all aspects of your Operation significantly: Global Issues, People, and Infrastructure. You need to research and have clarity on these issues before embarking on your entrepreneurial journey. They should come before you dive into prototype development and testing.

The Product section—which included the Product Definition Exercise and the Prototype / Initial Product Development Plan—showed you how to test your business idea and move forward if appropriate.

Chapter VI:
Review, Assess, and Choose Your Next Move

The Founder's Manifest has brought to your attention the importance of your founder role and the need to prepare yourself before embarking on an entrepreneurial journey.

You now recognize that you hold great responsibility and wield immense power—as founder and product originator. You've learned that, while your product idea and business model may evolve, the constant is you. Founder competency—including self-reliance—is essential. You are the one who is always accessible to you for support, troubleshooting, problem-solving, and moving your venture along.

You've taken note that a great idea alone does not guarantee financial success. You've recognized that product development is an integral part of a larger operation. It's imprudent to start by focusing all your energy on your product and ignoring the big picture.

The Founder's Manifest has introduced you to an integrated mindset and approach that help you: 1) develop, lead, and grow as a founder; 2) hire the right people, create the appropriate culture, and build your team; and 3) establish the infrastructure, systems, and processes that support your prototype development phase and your operation as it expands.

It's all about execution. That's why the more qualified and prepared you are, the higher the chance you will succeed. No singular startup model works for all; each venture is a trial-and-error voyage of adjustment and refinement. There's no "right age" to become an entrepreneur. The right time for you is when you feel ready. Hopefully, this is when you feel that: 1) all parts of your life—mind, body, heart, and spirit—are in good if not excellent shape, and 2) you are well positioned with resources to integrate your startup's life into your daily life.

After you've thought, researched, defined, and articulated, you'll be at a place where you have the means to make informed decisions. When you're ready, the next questions should help you identify where you are and decide your next move.

The Integrated You

At the start of your founder development, you took a Snapshot of Where You Are Today in Chapter IV. Review the answers you provided. Now that you've spent time reflecting, articulating, researching, and completing various exercises, let's see where you are today.

Exercise 64: A Snapshot of Where You Are Today, Post-Introspection and Integration

1. What new awareness have you acquired about yourself (sources of influence, habits, beliefs, and untapped skills), about your new business idea, and/or about your venture? List 3-5 useful insights have you acquired.

2. How have your insights, priorities, and goals for this year and next year changed? What are your revisions?

3. Knowing what you do now about how to develop your founder role and how to prepare for your startup, do you still feel pulled

toward your new business idea? Is it still compelling? Is this a must-do?

4. Envision what your daily routine will look like, how your start-up life will fit into the rest of your personal life.

5. The entrepreneurial voyage is a life-changing experience. Are you ready to transform your life?

6. What conditions need to be in place in order for you to feel ready to start this venture?

Founder Readiness		
Area	Condition that needs to be in place	Assess your readiness: (1 = not ready; 2 = almost ready, but need to accomplish a few tasks / learn new skills; 3 = ready to start)
Mind		
Body		
Spirit		
Heart		
Finance		

The Founder Section

Review Founder Competency:
- **Core action skills**: initiate, plan, execute, solve, and lead.
- **Core management skills**: self-management, time management, communication, relationship management, project management, stress management, crisis management, and financial management.
- **Core qualities**: self-awareness, self-reliance, discernment, adaptability, steadfastness, perseverance, optimism, and empathy.
- **Financial preparedness**
- **Industry experience**
- **Survival skills**

Exercise 65: Assess Your Readiness in the Founder Role

1. What core qualities, skills, sources of power, habits, and insights are helping you feel most confident, most ready to proceed as founder?

Factor (quality / skill / habit)	Examples that show you are in top form
1.	
2.	
3.	

2. What recurrent challenges and new issues (those that emerged during your Introspection exercises) do you need to keep in mind as you start the venture?

Factor (quality / skill / habit)	What you need to monitor
1.	
2.	
3.	

3. What core qualities, skills, and habits do you still need to develop or refine BEFORE starting your venture?

Factor (quality / skill / habit)	What you need to develop
1.	
2.	
3.	

4. Identify three goals that you want to accomplish in order to build your worth as founder.

5. Review your financial preparedness.

6. Identify three factors that might derail you during the first two years if you are not careful.

7. Envision your worst-case scenario: business failure. How will you move forward? What cushions will you have in place for yourself?

8. Review your Survival Kit. What physical tools, what intangible tools are your must-haves?

9. How qualified do you feel today, after introspection and integration?
    - Not qualified; still have to research and reflect some more
    - Somewhat qualified and need to develop some essential skills
    - Qualified and ready to start.

10. Create your short To-Do List. Set clear goals for your first and second years. Assign yourself weekly and monthly tasks. Focus and execute.

11. Monitor your progress frequently. Make time to review your personal achievements, as well as your founder's goals.
    - Rate your performance and take note of areas to be refined or strengthened.
    - Take note of lessons learned and insights gained.
    - Update your goals and start anew.

The Startup Section

Assess your readiness for your entire operation and product development. As founder, you are architect of your product and business. This book has given you a framework for your responsibilities as Product Developer for your idea as well as Founder for your business. After you've set groundwork, review the following questions.

Exercise 66: Assess Your Readiness for Operation and Product Development

1. Rate your readiness to create a blueprint for your operation that will support your product's development and expansion.

Founder Readiness		
Area	Condition that needs to be in place	Assess your readiness: (1 = not ready; 2 = almost ready, but need to accomplish a few tasks / learn new skills; 3 = ready to start)
Global issues		
People		
Infrastructure		

2. As Product Originator and Developer, how ready do you feel to begin your product research and testing?

Product Readiness		
Area	Condition that needs to be in place	Assess your readiness: (1 = not ready; 2 = almost ready, but need to accomplish a few tasks / learn new skills; 3 = ready to start)
Research: product idea, customers, markets, etc.		
Prototype development resources: design, materials, equipment, etc.		
Talent resources		
Seed investment		

Remember the adage "Proper planning prevents poor performance." The more qualified and self-reliant you are, the more prepared you will be to troubleshoot and solve your challenges without waiting for help to arrive because help doesn't always arrive. The more qualified and self-reliant you are, the more prepared you will be to face the entrepreneurial opportunities that you encounter and maximize them.

Your Master Checklist

You've spent substantial time reflecting, assessing, researching, and articulating your vision and plan. Create the following checklist to keep focused. Extract it for your business plan and investment deck—when you prepare for potential investors.

Exercise 67: Master Checklist

Master Checklist

1. Business Name and Description

2. Product
   - What does it do?
   - What problem / need does it address?
   - How much does it cost to create it?
   - How long does it take to create it?
   - How eco-friendly is it?
   - Who uses it?
   - Who pays for it?
   - How much will you charge to break even? To make a profit?
   - What is your expected profit margin?
   - How will you sell it?
   - Where will you sell it?

3. Crew
   - How well prepared are you as ship captain?
   - Where do you need help?
   - How will you obtain help?
   - How long will it take to get help?
   - How much are you paying for help?
   - What kind of people will be right for your crew?
   - What compensation structure will you have in place for your team?

4. Infrastructure
- What is your company culture?
- What is its organizational structure?
- What standards, systems, and processes do you have in place?

5. Finance
- How will you finance your prototype and later, startup operation?
- How much startup money will you have?
- How long before you run out of startup money, before your first sale?
- Have you researched all your financing options?
- Are you prepared to manage your accounts until you hire full-time help?

6. Your Critical Role
- How will you build your worth as founder through each phase?
- How will you manage yourself: stay in shape, keep yourself focused, and run a tight ship?
- How will you manage daily stress, unanticipated crises?
- How will you manage and lead your team?

7. Scenario Planning
- What are your venture's best-case, realistic-case, and worst-case scenarios?
- What's in your Survival Kit?
- How do you define venture success?
- What constitutes failure?
- What does your life look like beyond your startup up life?

Conclusion

At the start of this book, I stated that my goal was to help you move forward with your business idea.

You've spent time reading, reflecting, researching, and doing exercises. This has given you the opportunity to know yourself on mental, emotional, spiritual, physical, and financial levels. You now have the knowledge and insights to develop and grow as a founder. You also have a blueprint for a successful product launch and startup operation. Finally, you know how to create and customize your own manifest, which will serve as your guide, your go-to resource, and your Survival Kit.

Moving forward can mean that you're ready to prepare for your founder role; you're ready to start your business. Train yourself with *The Founder's Manifest*. Alternatively, moving forward can mean that you're not ready to strike out on your own or that the entrepreneurial path is not for you. Both are legitimate decisions, if informed.

I wish you the best, whether that means seeing your current career path in a new light or embarking on an entrepreneurial journey.

My-Tien Vo
San Francisco
California
March 2017

Notes

1. The New Shorter Oxford English Dictionary, Oxford University Press 1993.

2. Kauffman Index of Startup Activity 2016. Source: kauffman. org/~/media/kauffman_org/microsites/kauffman_index/startup_activity_2016/kauffman_index_startup_activity_national_trends_2016. pdf. (Accessed August 26, 2016).

3. SBA Statistics - U.S. Dept. of Commerce, Census Bureau, Busi-ness Dynamics Statistics; U.S. Department of Labor, Bureau of Labor Statistics, BED. Source: sba.gov/sites/default/files/sbfaq.pdf. (Accessed February 20, 2013).

4. Entrepreneur's Instant Startup Guide. Entrepreneur Magazine, March 2013.

5. History of banking. Source: en.wikipedia.org/wiki/History_of_banking. (Accessed August 25, 2012).

6. Claire Cain Miller, "In Google's Inner Circle, a Falling Number of Women," New York Times (August, 22 2012). Source: nytimes. com/2012/08/23/technology/in-googles-inner-circle-a-falling-number-of-women.html?pagewanted=2&_r=1&smid=pl-share&pagewanted=print. (Accessed March 12, 2014).

7. Bruce Upbin, "Facebook Buys Instagram for $1 Billion. Smart Arbitrage." Forbes (April 9, 2012). Source: forbes.com/sites/bruceupbin/2012/04/09/facebook-buys-instagram-for-1-billion-wheres-the-revenue/#5454a7dd447f. (Accessed April 11, 2012).

8. WhatsApp. Source: en.wikipedia.org/wiki/WhatsApp. (Accessed February, 2015).

9. John Koestler, "41 of the 2013 Fortune 500 Are Technology Companies." Venture Beat (May, 6 2013). Source: venturebeat.com/2013/05/06/41-of-the-fortune-500-companies-are-tech-companies-and-here-they-are/. (Accessed March 12, 2014).

10. The New Shorter Oxford English Dictionary, Oxford University Press 1993.

11. Worth: usefulness or importance, as to the world, to a person, or for a purpose. Source: dictionary.com. (Accessed August 25, 2012).

12. Alan Lakein, *How to Get Control of Your Time and Your Life* (Penguin Books USA Inc., 1973), 49.

13. Pareto Principle. Source: en.wikipedia.org/wiki/Pareto_principle. (Accessed August 25, 2012).

14. Power: ability to do or act; capability of doing or accomplishing something. Source: Dictionary.com. (Accessed August 25, 2012).

15. Geoff Smart and Randy Street, *Who - Solving Your #1 Problem* (ghSMART & Company, 2008). 148.

16. Market penetration. Source: en.wikipedia.org/wiki/Market_penetration. (Accessed August 25, 2012).

17. Marketing Mix. Source: en.wikipedia.org/wiki/Marketing_mix. (Accessed August 18, 2016).

18. "Uniqlo Chief Admits Defeat on Higher Pricing Strategy." Source: asia.nikkei.com/Business/Companies/Uniqlo-chief-admits-defeat-on-higher-pricing-strategy. (Accessed April 13, 2016).

19. Natural Selection: Charles Darwin & Alfred Russel Wallace. Source: evolution.berkeley.edu/evolibrary/article/history_14. (Accessed August 25, 2012).

20. Elisha Gray and Alexander Bell Telephone Controversy. Source: en.wikipedia.org/wiki/Elisha_Gray_and_Alexander_Bell_telephone_controversy. (Accessed August 25, 2012).

Founder Resources

Below are book series, titles, and links that you might find useful. Visit thefoundersmanifest.com for Resources updates.

Brilliant Series publish business books that cover a variety of subjects, from project management to marketing to branding to selling. (pearsoned.co.uk/bookshop/subject.asp?item=9655).

Nolo Series (nolo.com) publish informative business and legal books, which cover numerous topics, including *Legal Forms for Starting & Running a Business, Tax Savvy for Small Business, Contracts, and Working for Yourself.*

Small Business Administration (sba.gov) offers information on business structures, business licenses, loans and grants, business financials, and tax filings.

Ewing Marion Kauffman Foundation (kauffman.org) focuses on entrepreneurship.

TED Talks (ted.com) - A repository of information, insights, and inspiration.

Harvard Business Review (hbr.org) - Articles and books on entrepreneurship, business strategy, talent management, self management, productivity, marketing, etc.

Brand Strategy
- Catherine Kaputa, *You Are A Brand*
- Douglas B. Holt, *How Brands Become Icons*
- Doug Dvorak, *Build Your Own Brand*
- Scott Lerman, *Building Better Brand*
- Jeremy Miller, *Sticky Branding*

Business
- Jim Collins and Jerry I. Porras, *Built to Last: Successful Habits*
- *of Visionary Companies*
- Jim Collins, *Good to Great: Why Some Companies Make the Leap and Others Don't*
- Guy Kawasaki and Lindsey Filby, *The Art of the Start 2.0*

Communication and Presentation
- Amy Jen Su and Murial Maignan Wilkins, *Own The Room*
- Duarte offers an array of presentation templates (duarte.com/free-presentation-software-templates/)
- Deborah Gruenfeld on Power and Influence (womensleadership.stanford.edu/power)

Creativity
- Michael J. Gelb, *How to Think like Leonardo da Vinci*
- Brewster Ghiselin, *The Creative Process*
- Robert Grudin, *The Grace of Great Things*
- Rollo May, *The Courage to Create*

Crisis Management
- Harvard Business Essential, *Crisis Management: Mastering the Skills to Prevent Disasters*
- Steven Fink, *Crisis Communications: Planning for the Inevitable*
- Steve Tobak, *How to Manage a Crisis, Any Crisis* (cnet.com/news/how-to-manage-a-crisis-any-crisis/)

Finance
- Scott L. Girard, Jr., Michael F. O'Keefe, Marc A. Price, *Business Finance Basics*
- Mark Suster - Both Sides of the Table (bothsidesofthetable.com)
- Funders and Founders (fundersandfounders.com)
- Go4Funding (go4funding.com)
- How Startup Funding Works (fundersandfounders.com/how-funding-works-splitting-equity)

Leadership
- Terry R. Bacon, *Elements of Influence*
- Stephen Denning, *The Leader's Guide to Storytelling*
- Deborah Gruenfeld on Power and Influence (womensleadership.stanford.edu/power)
- Stephen E. Kohn and Vincent D. O'Connell, *6 Habits of Highly Effective Bosses*
- Derek Lidow, *How Savvy Entrepreneurs Turn Their Ideas Into Successful Enterprises*
- Nan S. Russell, *The Titleless Leader*

Marketing
- Mack Collier, *Think Like a Rock Start*
- Bruce David Keillor, *Marketing in the 21st Century and Beyond*
- Bruce David Keillor, *Understanding the Global Market*
- Marina Krakovsky, *The Middleman Economy*
- Rebecca Lieb, *Content Marketing*
- Keith A. Quesenberry, *Social Media Strategy*

Nonprofit
- Smith, Buckling & Associates, Inc. *The Complete Guide to Nonprofit Management*

Personal Development
- Marcus Aurelius, *Meditations* (Translated by Maxwell Staniforth)
- Joseph Campbell, *The Power of Myth*
- Joseph Campbell, *The Hero with a Thousand Faces*

- Chang Po-Tuan, *The Inner Teachings of Taoism* (Translated by Thomas Cleary)
- Stephen R. Covey, *The 7 Habits of Highly Effective People*
- Angela Duckworth, *Grit*
- Charles Duhigg, *Why We Do What We Do in Life and Business*
- Carol S. Dweck, Ph.D., *Mindset - The New Psychology of Success*
- Daniel Goleman, *Emotional Intelligence*
- Robert Grudin, *The Grace of Great Things*
- Allen F. Harrison and Robert M. Bramson, Ph.D., *Styles of Thinking*
- Caroline Myss, *Archetypes*
- Carol Pearson, *Awakening the Heroes Within*
- MBTI 16 Personalities (16personalities.com)
- Thich Nhat Hanh, *Peace Is Every Step - The Path of Mindfulness in Everyday life*
- Lane Wallace, *Surviving Uncertainty*

Power
- Terry R. Bacon, *The Elements of Power: Lessons on Leadership and Influence*
- Deborah Gruenfeld on Power and Influence (womensleadership.stanford.edu/power)
- Nicholas H. Morgan, *Power Cues*
- Jeffrey Pfeffer, *Power - Why Some People Have It And Others Don't*

Project Management
- Scott Berkun, *The Art of Project Management*
- Kory Kogon, Suzette Blakemore, James Wood, *Project Management for the Unofficial Project Manager*

Sales
- Marion Luma Bream, *Women Make the Best Salesmen*
- Kim MacPherson, *Permission-based E-Mail Marketing That Works!*
- Tom Martin, *The Invisible Sale*
- Ron Willingham, *Authenticity – The Head, Heart, and Sould of Selling*

Social Entrepreneurship
- Robert J. Rosenthal and Greg Baldwin, *Volunteer Engagement 2.0*

Startups
- Best Pitches (bestpitchdecks.com)
- Bloomberg U.S. Startups Barometer (bloomberg.com/graphics/startup-barometer)
- Scott Duffy, *Launch!: The Critical 90 Days from Idea to Market*
- Funders and Founders (fundersandfounders.com)
- Richard Stim and Lisa Guerin, *Wow! I am in Business*
- Mark Suster - Both Sides of the Table (bothsidesofthetable.com)
- NY Times Entrepreneurship (nytimes.com/pages/business/small-business)
- OnStartups (onstartups.com)
- Noam Wasserman, *The Founder's Dilemmas*

Talent Management
- Lou Adler, *Hire With Your Head*
- Dr. Joy Bodzioch, *Catching the Wave of Workforce Diversity*
- Amy DelPo and Lisa Guerin, *Create Your Own Employee Handbook*
- Mary B. Holihan, *Human Resources for the Small Business Owner*
- Mark Murphy, *Hiring for Attitude*
- Geoff Smart and Randy Street, *Who - The A Method for Hiring*
- Brad Feld and Mahendra Ramshinghani, *Startup Boards*

Thinking and Decision-Making Process
- Rolf Dobelli, *The Art of Thinking Clearly*
- Charles Duhigg, *The Power of Habit*
- John S. Hammond, *Smart Choices*
- Joseph T. Hallinan, *Why We Make Mistakes*
- Daniel Kahneman, *Thinking, Fast and Slow*
- Allen F. Harrison and Robert M. Bramson, Ph.D., *The Art of Thinking*
- Jonah Lehrer, *How We Decide*
- Rod Judkins, *The Art of Creative Thinking*

Time Management / Productivity
- David Allen, *Getting Things Done* (gettingthingsdone.com)
- Robert Grudin, *Time and The Art of Living*
- Alan Lakein, *How to Get Control of Your Time and Your Life*
- Carson Tate (carsontate.com)

•••

About the Author

My-Tien Vo is a founder coach, startup consultant, and brand strategist who has worked closely with founders, co-founders, and startup teams from various industries. They include construction, education, electrical, healthcare, hospitality, legal, nonprofit, professional services, real estate, retail, and technology. She has been immersed in the startup landscape since 1998—as founder, co-founder, product manager, brand strategist, content developer, founder coach, team builder, crisis manager, e-commerce director, and researcher.

Her work with founders has led to many successful launches and also a share of stalled operations. As an integral member of many startup teams, Vo has had first-hand experience of what works and what doesn't work. She felt compelled to share her entrepreneurial insights after one of her startups failed—in spite of possessing many winning attributes. What began as an essay for her blog has evolved into *The Founder's Manifest,* the first guide to founder development.

The Founder's Manifest presents an integrated mindset and approach to help aspiring entrepreneurs develop Founder Competency—skills and qualities needed to increase their chances of success with both product launch and startup operation.

Prior to embarking on her entrepreneurial path, Vo worked for an investment bank, an international management consulting firm, wireless service providers, and a family-owned business. Her corporate experiences proved a valuable asset to her startup endeavors. Vo earned a B.A. with Honors from Brown University and a M.A.L.D from The Fletcher School of Law and Diplomacy.